WAINWRIGHT
ON
THE PENNINE WAY

Also by A. Wainwright and Derry Brabbs

FELLWALKING WITH WAINWRIGHT
18 of the author's favourite walks in Lakeland

WAINWRIGHT'S COAST TO COAST WALK

WAINWRIGHT
ON
THE PENNINE WAY

with photographs by
DERRY BRABBS

Michael Joseph – London

CONTENTS

First published in Great Britain by Michael Joseph Limited
27 Wrights Lane, London W8 5TZ
June 1985
Second impression June 1985
Third impression November 1986

Wainwright A.
  Wainwright on the Pennine Way
  1. Walking — England — Pennine Way — Guide-
books   2. Pennine Way (England) — Guide-books
  I. Title
  796.5′ 1′09428   DA670.P4
                         ISBN 0 7181 2429 4 (hardback)
                         ISBN 0 7181 2838 9 (paperback)

Filmset by BAS Printers Ltd, Over Wallop, Hampshire
Printed and bound in Spain by Graficromo S.A., Cordoba.

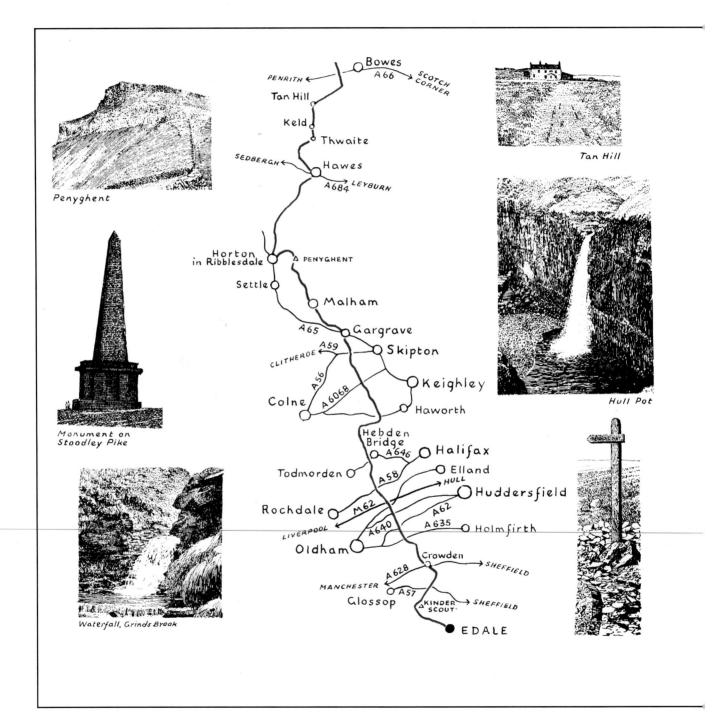

Bowes

PENRITH ← A66 → SCOTCH CORNER

Tan Hill

Keld

Thwaite

SEDBERGH ← Hawes
A684 → LEYBURN

Horton in Ribblesdale

△ PENYGHENT

Settle

Malham

A65

Gargrave

CLITHEROE ← A59
A56
A6068

Skipton

Keighley

Colne

Haworth

Hebden Bridge

A646

Halifax

Todmorden

Elland

A58

→ HULL

Huddersfield

Rochdale

M62

A62

A635 → Holmfirth

LIVERPOOL ←

A640

Oldham

Crowden → SHEFFIELD

A628

MANCHESTER ←

A57

△ KINDER SCOUT → SHEFFIELD

Glossop

● EDALE

Penyghent

Monument on Stoodley Pike

Waterfall, Grinds Brook

Tan Hill

Hull Pot

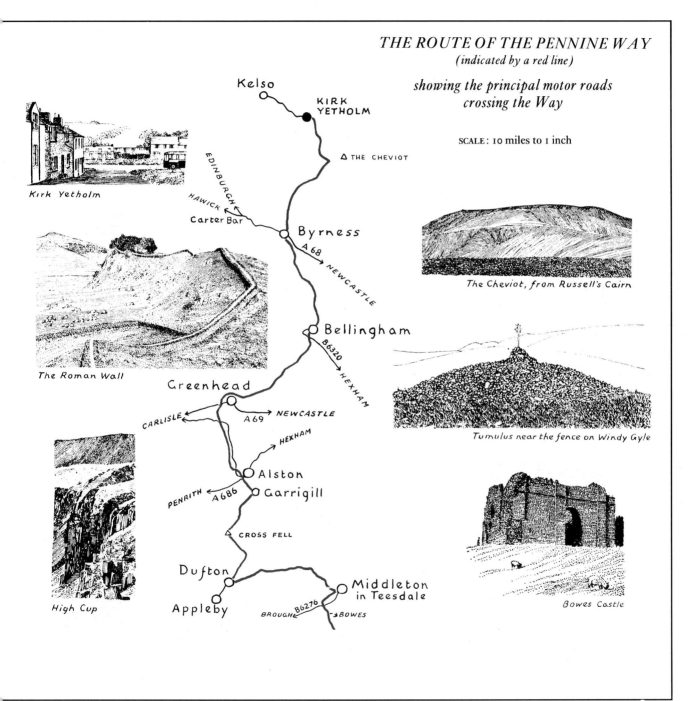

THE ROUTE OF THE PENNINE WAY
(indicated by a red line)

showing the principal motor roads crossing the Way

SCALE: 10 miles to 1 inch

Kelso

KIRK YETHOLM

△ THE CHEVIOT

EDINBURGH

HAWICK

Carter Bar

Byrness

A 68

NEWCASTLE

Bellingham

B6320

HEXHAM

Greenhead

CARLISLE

A 69 NEWCASTLE

HEXHAM

Alston

PENRITH A 686 Garrigill

△ CROSS FELL

Dufton

Appleby

BROUGH B6276 BOWES

Middleton in Teesdale

Kirk Yetholm

The Roman Wall

High Cup

The Cheviot, from Russell's Cairn

Tumulus near the fence on Windy Gyle

Bowes Castle

INTRODUCTION

THE Pennines are a range of high moorlands extending from Derbyshire to Hadrian's Wall and forming a natural barrier along the length of northern England. They are the main watershed of the region, the rivers flowing from their western slopes being destined for the Irish Sea and those flowing eastwards finding their way to the North Sea. The terrain is wild and lonely almost everywhere, without habitations except for an occasional isolated farmstead and providing pasture for sheep only where the grazing is not too coarse and sour. The area is largely used for water conservation, many of the upper valleys having impounding reservoirs, and parts have been adapted for forestry, but these operations contribute nothing to mellow the stark desolation all around. Where there are extensive tracts of heather, there is grouse shooting and public access is restricted. Roads cross the range, slender ribbons of tarmac that take advantage of gaps and depressions in the skyline and climb through harsh and hostile landscapes and are often snowbound in winter. The Pennines do not compromise: they are a wilderness of rough grasses and mosses and wastes of naked peat and outcropping rocks, with few landmarks to guide the traveller on foot, whose progress along the broad and featureless moors is further hindered by expanses of marshy ground. . . . This is a no-man's-land. Or was, until walkers were given a right of continuous access from one end of the range to the other: a challenging expedition undertaken by thousands of adventurers every year, the full traverse being a memorable experience. This route is the Pennine Way.

The Pennine Way was a happy inspiration of Mr Tom Stephenson, later to be Secretary of the Ramblers' Association, who suggested in 1935 the creation of a public footpath along the length of the Pennines that would be free from trespass and provide a continuous long-distance walk. His proposal extended beyond the Pennines to the Cheviot Hills and the Scottish border, a route of around 270 miles. It was a novel suggestion, for no other plan for a right of way for walkers over such a distance had ever previously been put forward, and it received enthusiastic support. But there were many difficulties to overcome, and only after many years of patient and protracted negotiations with private and public landowners, and much abortive discussion in Parliament, were all the necessary concessions obtained and the route given official blessing. On 24 April 1965, thirty years after the birth of the idea, the establishment of the Pennine Way was celebrated at a meeting of 2000 outdoor enthusiasts on Malham Moor, and the first long-distance footpath in England came into being. Tom Stephenson, who had worked assiduously for the completion of the project, was present on the occasion, his imaginative conception realised at last. He had served the cause of walkers well. The Pennine Way is his memorial.

As outlined in my Note on page 213, this book is not intended as a step-by-step guide to the Pennine Way, but rather as a souvenir for those who have completed the walk and a refresher of memories. It gives a general impression of the territory covered, and in particular draws attention to outstanding natural features of the landscape, archaeological remains and buildings of special interest met along the Way or reached by a short detour off-route: the highlights of the journey. In essence, it is a book of photographs, always more evocative of memories than the written word could ever be. The book will have a use also for those who are planning a closer acquaintance with the Pennine Way by giving a foretaste of the terrain to be expected and the atmosphere of the surroundings.

In arrangement both narrative and photographs describe the Way from south to north, this being the direction usually followed, having the advantage of the prevailing weather coming from behind. The starting point is Edale in Derbyshire.

The Old Nag's Head Inn, Edale

Below *The packhorse bridge, Edale*

EDALE is a rural parish of small farming communities at the foot of Kinder Scout, popularly known as The Peak, in northern Derbyshire, its name being applied also to the principal concentration of buildings, although few in number, along and at the end of a short side road leading off the main road through the Vale of Edale. Having a church, an inn, a shop and a café, and the privilege of a railway and a still-operative railway station, it qualifies for the status of village, albeit a small one.

Edale had long been known to walkers from Manchester and Sheffield and the neighbouring districts as a springboard for moorland excursions before being given prominence over a much wider field by its adoption as the starting point of the Pennine Way. Since then it has become a place of popular resort, attracting not only walkers intent on the Pennine Way but others who have no such ambitions yet find the immediate surroundings pleasant for picnics and short rambles. On summer weekends, the parking spaces for cars are fully occupied. Edale, once quiet and secluded, has become busy and often noisy.

The Pennine Way starts at the cluster of buildings named Grindsbrook Booth centred around the Old Nag's Head Inn and goes forward along the valley of Grinds Brook due north. There is an alternative start to the west by way of Upper Booth and Jacob's Ladder, officially recommended in bad weather to avoid the trek across the featureless Kinder plateau beyond the head of Grindsbrook Clough, the two routes meeting at Kinder Downfall. But wise counsel advises that neither route should be attempted in bad weather. In any case, the main route is becoming better defined underfoot by the tread of many boots and the suggested alternative has lost its earlier slight advantages. But the Kinder plateau remains, and will always remain, a confusing area in adverse weather conditions in spite of way-marking by cairns. Pray for a day of clear visibility.

Before setting forth in earnest, a narrow packhorse bridge crossing Grinds Brook, off-route but only a minute's walk east of the inn, is well worth a visit and the first camera study of the day.

Grindsbrook Clough

Below *Kinder Gates*

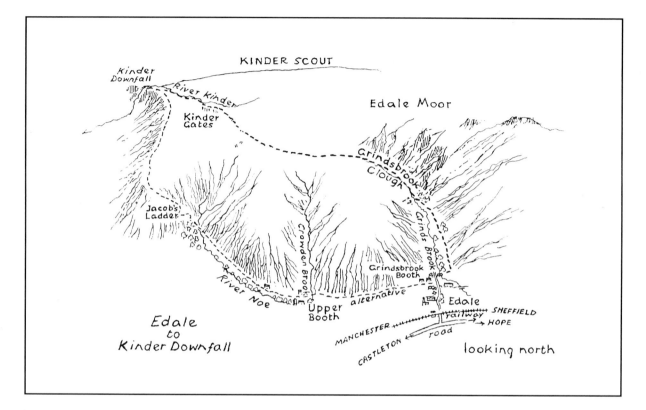

Having tightly girded up the loins and assumed a look of resolute determination, walkers bound for the Scottish border start their long journey by proceeding along the lane at the side of the inn to a Pennine Way guidepost that points to a path going down to a wooden bridge over Grinds Brook, here in a dell amongst trees. Across the bridge there are the first evidences of erosion caused by the passage of many boots, the original path having been scoured away and substituted by a flight of steps leading up to easier ground and a good path in the field above. This path, much used and blazed to the width of a cart track, heads very pleasantly up the valley, Grinds Brook being down on the left between steepening slopes, its swift course splashed white by waterfalls. After a short mile the path inclines west to enter the grim portals of Grindsbrook Clough, a rough tumble of boulders within narrow confines. Here the imprints of the sandals of genteel sightseers come to an end: heavy boots are needed for the arduous scramble upwards with the stream as companion. At the top of the gorge, having already attained an altitude of 2000 ft, the scene ahead changes dramatically to an open and uninviting landscape of peat mosses, the flat wilderness of the Kinder plateau. Route selection now needs care, the general direction being north-west until the headwaters of the River Kinder are reached, the name being an ambitious one for a sluggish trickle. It has, however, carved a defined channel through the wastes of peat, and can be followed through the rocky defile of Kinder Gates without possibility of straying, to the edge of the western escarpment of Kinder Scout and the abrupt and spectacular declivity of Kinder Downfall.

Weathered rocks on Kinder Scout

Below *Kinder Downfall*

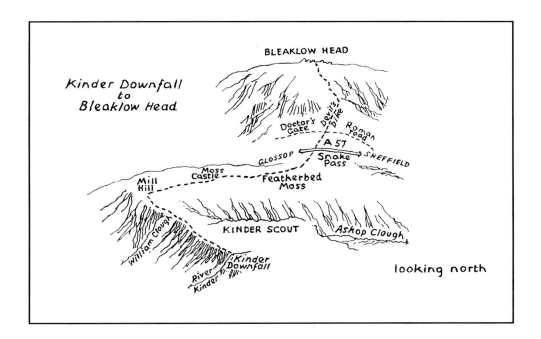

BEYOND the Downfall, the route continues in a north-westerly direction across the edge of the escarpment, the walking here being simple and straightforward and made palatable by extensive views to the west. In total contrast, the plateau stretches away to the eastern horizon in a maze of peaty channels known locally as groughs (pronounced gruffs), rough hummocks and marshy hollows that capture and hold the rain, and occasional outcroppings of gritstone smoothed by the weather into strange and often grotesque shapes. Nothing moves in this upland wilderness: all is silent, eerie, seemingly a dead landscape. Yet there is life here. It is a habitat of grouse and curlew, and on the ground flourish cotton grass and heather and mosses, with patches of bilberry and the rare cloudberry, adding colour and seasonal beauty to the drab surroundings. The terrain, everywhere difficult to traverse, rises very slightly to the insignificant summit of Kinder Scout, at 2088 ft. One wonders how this flat tableland came to earn its name as The Peak. Nothing less like a peak can be imagined.

Western buttresses of Kinder Scout

Peat groughs

The path along the escarpment skirts the top of William Clough, where a track goes down to Hayfield, and then rises to Mill Hill, 1761 ft. Here there is an open aspect to the east, the abrupt northern edge of the Kinder plateau being seen above the deep and widening valley of Ashop Clough. Here too the route changes direction sharply, heading north-east to Featherbed Moss, a prospect not to be anticipated with pleasure.

The section from Mill Hill (no mill and not much hill) to Moss Castle (all moss and no castle) is dreary and without landmarks. Earlier Pennine Wayfarers, before a path was formed, were given confidence that they were heading in the right direction by a line of fence posts connecting one with the other. Beyond Moss Castle, conditions underfoot deteriorate as the spongy morass of Featherbed Moss is reached. The Moss is a mess. Progress is made across it by slithering down and struggling out of innumerable channels in the peat. Nobody has a kind word to say about Featherbed Moss, and no wonder, for it does nothing to earn it. But all bad things come to an end and in due course there comes into sight, almost like a mirage, a stream of cars and lorries travelling at speed across the moor ahead, obviously on a smoother surface than the squelchy quagmire around. This traffic indicates the presence of the Snake Road, but much arduous effort remains before the welcome strip of tarmac is reached. Walkers don't like motor roads but they will be glad to find their feet on this one.

Featherbed Moss

Doctor's Gate   *Devil's Dike*

The Snake Road (A.57) is a principal artery linking Manchester and Sheffield and the only direct road route between the two cities. The road climbs to 1680 ft at its exposed summit and is usually the first Pennine crossing to be blocked by winter snowfalls. The name seems to be derived, not from its sinuous curves as may reasonably be supposed, but from a snake featured in the coat of arms of the Cavendish family, the landowners at the time of the construction of the road in 1821. The engineer in charge of the work was the renowned Thomas Telford.

The sheer bliss of walking on a smooth surface is short-lived, for the Pennine Way continues directly across the road, now happily on easier ground. The next objective is Bleaklow Head, the sprawling mass of high moorland now in sight. If perchance it is not in sight, due to a covering of mist, the wisdom of going further should be debated: it is a hostile beast in bad weather. The last opportunity for such a decision occurs where traces of a Roman road cross the path: this, one of a network of Roman roads in Derbyshire, linked the forts of Melandra at Glossop and Navio near Bradwell. It becomes very distinct as it descends, left to Glossop and right to the Snake Inn, retaining original paving in sections. If overnight accommodation is sought at either place, this Roman route is greatly to be preferred to the busy A.57. This old track is known as Doctor's Gate, so named after Dr John Talbot of Glossop, a regular traveller on it in the sixteenth century.

After crossing Doctor's Gate the continuation of the Way is indicated by a long, straight trench cut through the peat and known as Devil's Dike, which is followed across a flat and featureless moor to its terminus half a mile forward.

Beyond the end of Devil's Dike, the ground steepens and a few isolated boundary posts serve as way-marks over a rising desert of peat groughs, heathery hummocks and boggy hollows. Progress is slow and made only by a series of trials and errors in a confusing terrain. Reliance cannot be placed in following bootmarks in the mud, which may be the wandering imprints of lost pilgrims. The best advice is to keep plodding upwards and the highest point of Bleaklow Head will inevitably be reached. Deep valleys fall away on both sides during the ascent and are to be avoided by persisting along the ill-defined and rising ridge between. After a weary mile, the Wain Stones come into sight, these being a cluster of strange gritstone rocks, and the gradients ease into the flat top of Bleaklow Head, a welcome oasis of sand and pebbles.

My own experiences on Bleaklow were dreadful, one on a day of sluicing rain and another of drifting mist. Many other walkers have reported this hill as an unfriendly and cheerless place, and rescues have been necessary. But when I wrote some years ago that nobody loved Bleaklow and that those who got on it were glad to get off it, my words brought a stinging rebuke from a Huddersfield man who told me that he and his companions often walked over Bleaklow and were very fond of it, that it was quite wrong of me to malign it and that I should apologise. I did so without changing my opinion. . . . Well, I suppose everything, however unattractive, is loved by somebody.

Bleaklow Head

The summit cairn on Bleaklow Head stands at 2060 ft, overtopping all else around, and has extensive views of industrial Lancashire and a wide prospect over Yorkshire but distance robs them of detail and they are seen only as narrow strips above miles of sprawling moorland. Looking back, there is a last sighting of Kinder Scout filling the southern horizon, but of more immediate interest is the dark mass of Black Hill across the deep and as yet unseen valley of Longdendale and identified by the television masts of Holme Moss. This is the next stage of the journey.

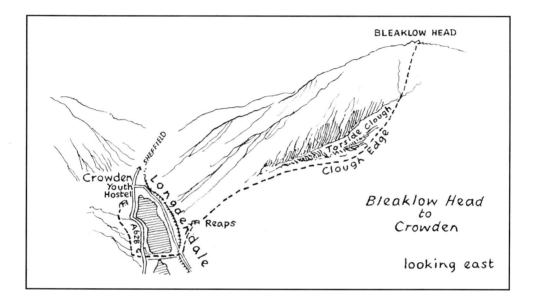

AT Bleaklow Head, the main watershed goes east and is forsaken, the route now turning north of west and declining over easier ground. A confluence of streams is forded and the long curving escarpment of Clough Edge traversed high above the wild and rugged hollow of Torside Clough. There are glimpses of Longdendale along here, and although it is nice to see green in the landscape again, the valley does not look too inviting, its floor being occupied by reservoirs and lines of communication. Good paths on Bleaklow are too rare to be ignored, and one develops along Clough Edge to simplify the descent into Longdendale. This is reached at Reaps Farm, the first habitation met since leaving Edale. From here, a farm road leads to crossings of a secondary road, B.6105, and a railway; beyond, a walk along the embankment of Torside Reservoir reaches the main road through the valley, the A.628, also linking Manchester and Sheffield.

Longdendale is a good example of a once-lovely valley made ugly by man's intervention. Crowded in the narrow confines are a series of reservoirs, two roads, telegraph poles, railway lines and pylons. Sweetness has turned sour. Rural silence has been drowned by urban noise. Rhododendrons planted near the reservoirs to add beauty to the scene fail to do so. Nothing could. Even the soggy Featherbed Moss had a certain shy charm but Longdendale has none at all. Nature has been badly let down here.

Longdendale has one thing in its favour: it offers overnight accommodation and all who have trudged the fifteen rough miles from Edale should accept the opportunity. The next stage of the journey is no less inhospitable than Kinder and Bleaklow and a sore trial for legs already tired. It is usual to seek a night's lodgings at the Crowden Youth Hostel, a hostel out of the ordinary, converted from six cottages and reconstructed to cater not only for members but also for any passing travellers, providing refreshments and private rooms. It was opened in 1965 with the blessing of the Peak Park Planning Board and the government, and has proved a boon for walkers on the Pennine Way. The hostel is situated a mile and a half along the A.628, east from the point on the road reached after crossing the reservoir embankment, but this very busy highway can be avoided by field paths.

Torside Clough

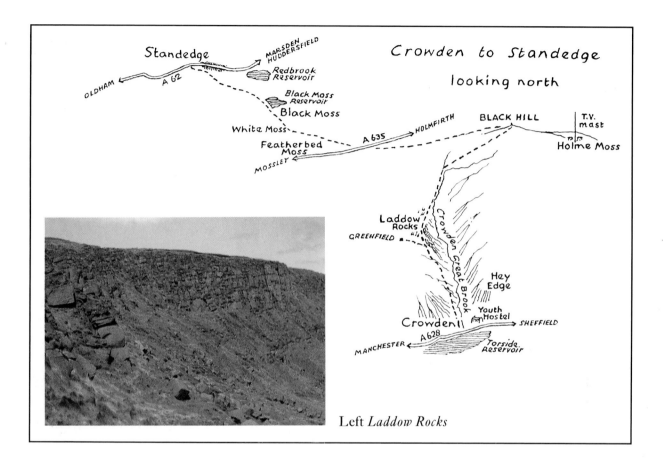

Left *Laddow Rocks*

NOW for Black Hill. And a warning. If Bleaklow is a beast in bad weather Black Hill is a brute in any weather. Walkers must be prepared for a tough and gruelling trek through glutinous slime. Girding up the loins is of no avail. Iron determination is needed. And a companion with strong arms.

The original route from Crowden climbed steeply up Hey Edge behind the hostel and then aimed directly for the summit over mosses and peat. In 1966, this section was revised in favour of a more circuitous route passing over Laddow Rocks and keeping on the west side of Crowden Great Brook to its headwaters and finally making a pathless beeline to the summit. In my opinion, the Hey Edge route is preferable.

The officially approved route now uses a good path leaving Crowden and rising across the moors to Greenfield, but departs from it when level with the top of Laddow Rocks, when a track along the edge of the crags is followed north. Laddow Rocks are conspicuous during the ascent from Crowden and are impressive at close range. These cliffs are a well-known gritstone climbing ground, a favourite resort of men with ropes, and provide spectacular glimpses from the rim of the escarpment to Crowden Great Brook far below.

Black Hill

The track continues over the top of Laddow Rocks and comes alongside the upper reaches of Crowden Great Brook, which is followed to its source at a confluence of streams in a hollow. This is where the pleasure starts for masochists, but others with no inclination towards self-punishment will find no joy in the next hour.

At this point the summit of Black Hill is a mile distant north-east but not yet in sight. This mile is gruesome. There is a slight ascent to the squelchy morass of Grains Moss, beyond which the gradient eases into a plateau of peat, naked and unashamed and cut into by innumerable little channels where water collects, making progress arduous. Vegetation has been stripped away; all around is an interminable and stagnant mudflat. One does not walk along here, one flounders. Underfoot all is black and slippery and treacherously soft. . . . Then, when hope is fast fading, the television mast on Holme Moss comes into sight and the triangulation column marking the summit of Black Hill can be discerned gleaming white in a jet landscape. There is a temptation to rush to greet it, but this is physically impossible. Boots can only be slowly dragged one after another. The last hundred yards are the worst of all.

Black Hill is well named. The broad top really is black. It is not the only hill with a summit of peat but no other shows such a desolate and hopeless quagmire to the sky. Nature fashioned it but had no plans for clothing it. Nothing can grow in this acid wasteland. There is no root-hold in this sea of ooze. In the flutings and ripplings of the surface of the peat dunes, caused by the action of wind and rain, there is a certain weird beauty, a patterned sculpturing beyond the skill of man. But it is a dreadful place in bad weather, and dangerous after heavy rain.

My most frightening experience in a long lifetime of fellwalking occurred here. I was crossing a small wet channel of peat that seemed innocuous enough, when suddenly my boots sank out of sight followed by several inches of each leg, more inches being submerged as I tried to extricate myself. Desperate struggles made matters worse. I was firmly anchored in bottomless mud, appearing as a man with both legs amputated below the knees. I was trapped in a vice, helpless to break free. Fortunately on this occasion I had a companion, but all his frantic tuggings were in vain. By the rarest of chances, a Park Ranger was sitting by the triangulation column, within hailing distance, and four tugging arms proved more effective and I was pulled out like a cork out of a bottle. . . . At that time I weighed sixteen stone which must have added to my distress, and sylphlike pedestrians might be spared such ordeals but, however light of foot, Black Hill should always be trodden with care.

The Ordnance column stands at 1908 ft on a tiny island of firm ground in the middle of a sea of black mud, and the surveyors who built it must have been mightily relieved when their measurements confirmed that this green oasis was in fact the highest point, for in no other place on the wide summit could a solid footing be found. It is perhaps unkind to suspect that there are a few slightly higher surfaces nearby.

The mound forming the actual top is named Soldiers Lump on some Ordnance maps, this name being derived from the visits of the triangulation party, the Corps of Royal Engineers. An examination of the mound in 1841 revealed the framework timbers for the 36″ Great Ramsden theodolite used in the original triangulation, which began in 1784.

The summit of Black Hill

From the top of Black Hill the main route heads north-west, varying little in direction for the next six miles to Standedge. An alternative bad-weather route also leaves the summit north-east, making a detour through the Wessenden valley: this alternative is longer and has lost some of its appeal since facilities for refreshment and meals at Wessenden Lodge, midway, were withdrawn. The fact that a bad-weather route was thought necessary here suggests that there is difficult terrain ahead along the main route, and so it will be proved.

But after conquering Black Hill, nothing is likely to deter walkers with stout hearts, who will resolutely face the north-west. The descent at first is through a maze of peat hags, but gradually the ground smooths, relatively speaking, and amongst vegetation again, the way down, aided by a few posts and cairns, is at least tolerable and even made pleasant in places by the white stars of the lovely cloudberry and cotton-grass.

Cloudberry

Cotton-grass

Peat groughs, Featherbed Moss

Tarmac is reached at a boundary stone on the exposed A.635, here crossing a desolation of peat moors between Mossley and Holmfirth and carrying the Manchester–Barnsley bus service. A mile to the west from this point is a site with sad associations: the tragic scene of the burials in the 'Bodies on the Moor' murders in 1966.

The Way continues across the road, and it will be noted with apprehension that the next section is another Featherbed Moss, which repeats the horrors of the first in even more virulent form. A labyrinth of peaty sponges and wet hollows must now be negotiated, the soft ground being cut into by deep groughs. These dark channels, floored with sand and pebbles and trickles of water, provide the easiest walking although they wind about in all directions and tempt footsteps to stray from a direct course.

Featherbed Moss merges into White Moss, and White Moss merges into Black Moss, conditions under-foot gradually becoming rather easier with heather relieving the drab surroundings. Cairns appear along the route, which here is following the main watershed between the Mersey and the Ouse, streamlets slowly winding away in both directions although much of the rain falling on this featureless expanse prefers to stay where it falls. Views open up, the small town of Diggle appearing down on the left. At Black Moss Reservoir, a haunt of gulls, the Wessenden alternative joins in. The reservoir embankment is crossed and then the walking becomes easy compared with what has just been endured and may even be described as enjoyable. A slight rise is succeeded by a gentle decline, with vistas opening ahead of Redbrook Reservoir, a haunt of yachts, and the busy A.62 highway. These signs of human activity are welcome after the many miles of lifeless moors. A good track, formerly a packhorse road, is joined, and this runs along the rim of Standedge Cutting, where a great slice has been carved out of the moor to provide a passage for the road, which is reached at its highest point.

Standedge is one of the busiest Pennine crossings. The A.62 links Manchester and Huddersfield and is a main artery of the industrial zones east and west of the Pennines, and there are continuous streams of heavy traffic and a bus service. The wonders of Standedge, however, are underground. This is an area of notable civil engineering works carried out in the nineteenth century. Directly beneath the road and 600 ft below the surface are three tunnels: the longest canal tunnel in the country (5415 yds) and two railway tunnels, each over three miles in length, emerging at Diggle and Marsden.

There was formerly a roadside transport café where the Way crosses the A.62, but it was destroyed by fire some years ago, robbing Wayfarers of a reward they have richly earned. Now, if meals or beds and breakfasts are sought, they will be found by a short stroll down the road to the west, or by a bus ride to Marsden. Boots, which by this time resemble slimy and shapeless lumps of mud, should in common decency be left outside any premises that are entered to avoid incurring the wrath of the proprietors and possible expulsion.

Standedge Cutting

Civilisation is all right in its way and has many advantages, but at Standedge is litter-strewn and noisy after the silence of the moors and it is a relief to cross the road and continue the journey to the uplands beyond and hear only the larks and the curlews, cheered by the promise of easier and more interesting territory ahead. At Standedge, twenty-six soggy miles out of Edale, the character of the terrain changes and the worst part of the journey is behind, and from here onwards the Pennine Way can be enjoyed.

I may have seemed unkind in my references to the Pennine hills thus far, but this does not indicate any bias against them. On the contrary I have a long affection for these bleak moorlands: they were the hills of my boyhood and youth. Assessment of their merits may be warped somewhat by a subsequent half-century spent amongst the far grander mountains of the Lake District, but of course I love them still. In fact, I have always maintained that every hill and every mountain is worth climbing, the only exception being Black Hill.

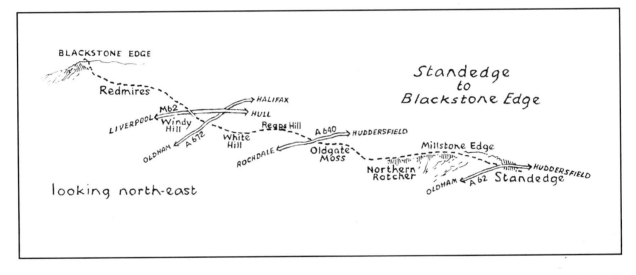

THE walk continues across the Standedge road, a short lane leading to a choice of two paths both of which climb gently to Millstone Edge, where in rather more exciting surroundings weathered rocks form a small escarpment.

A triangulation column crowns the highest point of Millstone Edge, along which the walking is delightful on a dry and firm surface of gravelly sand skirting the fringe of a vast peat moor, with open views to the west. The rock formations are interesting although too small and scattered for serious climbing, the escarpment being more imaginary than real. Two features are worthy of note on this simple promenade.

The Ammon Wrigley
Memorial Stone

Just beyond the column is the Ammon Wrigley Memorial Stone, identified by two tablets affixed to the face of a large rock. Ammon (1861–1946) was a revered writer and poet whose love of the countryside around his native Saddleworth was evident in all his works. The rock commemorating his name is the venue of an annual ceremony in his honour. A little further along the Edge is a conspicuous flat-topped rock adorned with a cairn and known locally as the Dinner Stone. It provides a natural table for a picnic lunch and, with a far-reaching prospect to the west, is an ideal spot for dining on a fine summer's day.

A mile further and still enjoying the rare pleasure of a dry and distinct path, the end of the escarpment is reached at the rocky outcrop of Northern Rotcher.

Millstone Edge

Above *Northern Rotcher*

Stone guide post

Beyond Northern Rotcher the path reverts to a more primitive state, winding over grass and heather to Oldgate Moss, where a view of the upper Colne valley opens up to the east; also prominently seen a mile north is a white building, Buckstones House, the scene of an unsolved double murder in 1903. This house stands on the A.640, the Rochdale–Huddersfield road, which is soon reached at a boundary stone. At this point, an old packhorse trail diverges to the right, heading for Marsden and typical of many such trade routes in use in medieval times. Centuries ago, long before the making of the motor roads across the Pennines, the considerable trade in merchandise between Lancashire and Yorkshire was carried by packhorses and carts travelling on made ways over the moors. These, where not converted into modern highways, can still be traced although now deteriorated by disuse into rutted grooves. The Marsden packhorse road still retains occasional stone posts as guides along the route.

It is no use waiting for a bus at the A.640 and there is no overnight accommodation within miles so this is no place to call a halt to the day's walk. The Way continues across the road with a slight ascent to Rapes Hill, the towering masts of the G.P.O. station on Windy Hill here coming into sight directly ahead. The route then makes a wide detour to the west, passing over White Hill, where feet will surely get wet when crossing the marshes surrounding the Ordnance column on its summit. Then follows a turn north and a gentle decline over peat and gravel beds to yet another road crossing, the A.672 linking Oldham and Halifax.

There is a succession of roads crossing the Pennines, most of them laid over peat mosses in desolate terrain without habitations, and I always found it an eerie experience when tramping at a snail's pace in absolute silence over the tangled wastes of heather and peat, to see suddenly ahead streams of traffic moving swiftly across the moor on roads that could not be seen until reached.

The A.672, which has a bus service, is reached at a county boundary stone and directly in front are the masts of the G.P.O. Wireless Telegraph Station.

Windy Hill Wireless Telegraph Station

The Pennine Way footbridge over the M.62

Across the A.672, the Way passes to the right of the masts and soon reaches the greatest of the roads, the Trans-Pennine motorway M.62, here in a deep cutting with a footbridge, provided especially for Pennine Way walkers, gracefully spanning the busy road below. The motorway was constructed in the late 1960s, after the route of the Pennine Way had been approved as a right of way, and the engineers were therefore under an obligation to make an overhead crossing.

Over the footbridge there is a slight incline to yet another juicy section: the extensive marsh of Redmires. This is a torment to the flesh, particularly the feet. Progress is squelchy and slow as the eyes search in vain for a few inches of firm ground on which to plant the next step. On the occasion of my visit, following heavy rain, the crossing of the marsh was a nightmare of apprehension. Depression assails the mind. Faint hearts will be tempted to give up the ghost and let life ebb away in this hopeless quagmire. It is all the more galling to see people enjoying themselves in yachts on Redmires Reservoir, half a mile east. Flounderers through this mess can be assured that there is nothing worse than Redmires to follow. This is the last of the ghastly morasses and from here on boots can be kept reasonably clean until the Scottish border is reached.

Survivors will ultimately reach drier ground as they approach the escarpment of Blackstone Edge in a sombre and gloomy environment of dark gritstone rocks. But, after Redmires, this is heaven.

The summit of Blackstone Edge

Blackstone Edge occupies a key position on the Pennine Way. Here matters change for the better. Left behind now are the dark peat moorlands, the marshes and the groughs that have so hindered progress thus far: ahead for the next hundred miles is much easier terrain for walking where a normal gait can be resumed and four miles an hour maintained. There is colour in the landscape ahead, green returning to add brightness to the scene and replacing the browns and blacks of the moors. And there are trees, which have been sorely missed. And from here onwards there are extensive views: the bare heights so far traversed have been broad and sprawling, restricting views on all sides, but now there will be variety and detail in the surroundings. And, best of all for walkers of a timid or gregarious disposition, the awesome sense of loneliness and the feeling of being solitary in a hostile environment, evaporate. People will be met, and habitations will never be far away; there will be shops and pubs, and the general atmosphere will be friendlier. Life comes good again on Blackstone Edge.

Blackstone Edge is a barrier between east and west and has historical associations concerned mainly with early lines of communication. There are evidences of packhorse and coach roads crossing the Edge centuries before the construction of the modern A.58, the best defined being a remarkable paved causeway attributed to the Romans. This is reached by walking north along the escarpment to the Aiggin Stone, obviously a guide post of great antiquity and bearing carvings of a cross and initials. On the occasion of my visit, the Stone had been dislodged and toppled over, but it is to be hoped that local antiquarians have since restored it to an upright position.

The Aiggin Stone

The causeway alongside is a wonderful relic of times long past, the paving being in pristine condition and of cart-width over a lengthy distance. On Ordnance maps, it is indicated as 'Roman Road, course of', but there has been much recent contention that the paving is not of Roman origin, the pattern of construction being more akin to that of the early packhorse roads and cart roads in use long before the Industrial Revolution called for better modes of transport. Discovery of Roman coins nearby supports the Roman theory and presumably their original road was later overlain with paving.

The causeway on Blackstone Edge

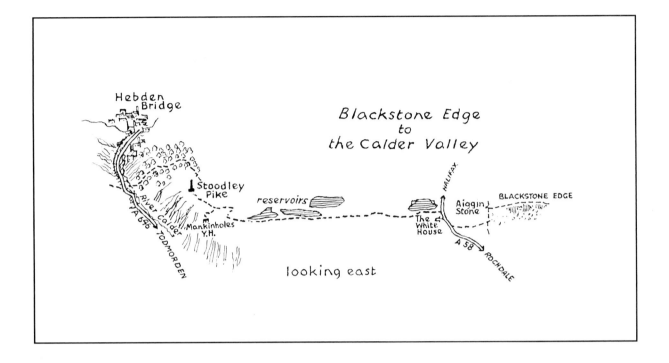

FROM the Aiggin Stone onwards for the next three miles the Pennine Way makes its first and only excursion wholly within Lancashire before returning to West Yorkshire. The causeway is followed down to a waterworks road, this then being used to reach the A.58 (Rochdale–Halifax bus service) near the White House, a long-established hostelry that presumably served the earlier coach road and now has a Hikers' Bar catering for walkers whose appearance is not too disreputable.

The White House

Just beyond the White House, the Way turns left along another waterworks road, and starts the easiest section of the Pennine Way, a level walk on the embankments of a succession of reservoirs constructed by Oldham Corporation. Here rapid progress can be made and is sheer bliss for those who like to stride out at speed. Ahead the deeply-inurned Calder Valley and the prominent monument on Stoodley Pike come into sight. After passing the last of the reservoirs, there is a return to moorland tracks as the Way turns east and then north to a cairn on Coldwell Hill. Beyond this, a flagged path, typical of many in this district goes down left to the Mankinholes Youth Hostel, a customary overnight halt for walkers entitled to this privilege, but non-members will continue their beeline to the monument, which becomes more imposing with every step.

The monument on Stoodley Pike

Below *View from Stoodley Pike to Heptonstall*

The towering obelisk on Stoodley Pike dominates the upper Calder Valley and is a landmark for miles around. It rises 120 ft above the moor and is massively built of blocks of the native millstone. It was constructed to commemorate the Peace of Ghent and the abdication of Napoleon in 1814 and has twice been restored after suffering collapse. The monument can be entered on the north side at ground level amongst threats of imminent doom daubed and carved on the walls by visitors, and a stone staircase spirals upwards in horrific darkness to a viewing balcony at the base of the obelisk. An inscribed tablet high above the entrance records, in badly weathered and barely decipherable lettering, the history of the monument. It commands a fine view of the valley, which from here, softened by distance, appears pleasantly rural and wooded with little sign of industry.

Lane in Callis Wood   Opposite *Hebden Bridge*

From Stoodley Pike, there is a circuitous descent to the Calder Valley, the final stages leading down a very pleasant lane through Callis Wood. It is a refreshing change to be amongst trees and twittering birds, but the enjoyment of this section is short-lived, ending abruptly in the squalid mess of the valley. For the first time since Longdendale, the Way comes down from high ground to cross a valley and, upon suddenly emerging from the avenue of trees, the eyes are assailed by the industrial blight immediately ahead: a stagnant canal, a dirty river, a very busy road and a railway are crowded side by side in a tangle of communications amongst rows of cottages and factories. The nose is assailed, too, the point of entry being between a pig farm and a sewage works. Clearly this is no place to linger. Mercifully the valley is narrow and the crossing brief to the continuation of the Pennine Way on the opposite side. But only a mile distant and quickly reached along the road (the A.646, carrying the Burnley–Halifax bus service) is the small town of Hebden Bridge. And Hebden Bridge repays a visit.

Attractively situated at the confluence of the River Calder and Hebden Water, and encompassed by hills, Hebden Bridge, although mainly industrial, has charm and character. Terraces of cottages rise one above another in tiers up the steep hillsides almost to the skyline, always reminding me of pictures I have seen of Tibetan monasteries. Factories crowd the valley bottom, there are shops in variety, and public gardens border the river. But of more immediate interest to Pennine Wayfarers will be the feeding of hungry mouths and the overnight resting of jaded limbs, and these necessary facilities are abundantly available. In fact, if itineraries permit, it is a good idea to enjoy a rest day at Hebden Bridge and to spend it on a gentle stroll, unburdened by rucksacks and other impediments apart from the camera, alongside Hebden Water to one of the most renowned beauty spots in the north of England, Hardcastle Crags.

The walk to Hardcastle Crags, especially in spring or autumn, is of bewitching beauty. Public footpaths accompany the course of Hebden Water upstream through lovely woodlands for some miles, and although the crags will probably be screened by foliage and not seen, every step of the walk is a joy. I remember that, when I was a boy, regular excursion trains ran from the towns of Lancashire and Yorkshire to Hebden Bridge specifically for visits to Hardcastle Crags. I could never afford the fare, but the name was magic. In those early days it was better known than the Lake District. Hardcastle Crags was a Mecca and many were the pilgrims.

The path to Hardcastle Crags

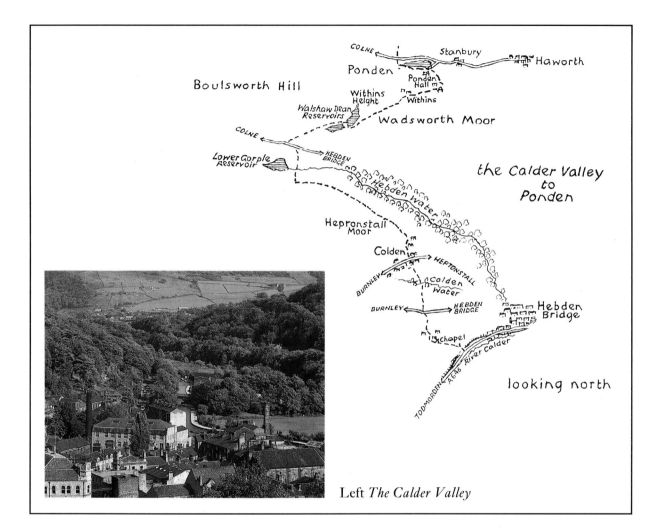

Left *The Calder Valley*

IT seems rather a pity that the route of the Pennine Way bypasses Hebden Bridge and Hardcastle Crags, thereby depriving walkers who are determined to follow the approved line and no other of a more interesting and beautiful alternative. But I suppose the main aim of the Way is to traverse the range of the Pennines by keeping to the high ground as much as possible. Those who have made the detour must therefore return along the A.646 to the point on the road reached after coming down from Callis Wood.

Across the road a lane rises to the ruins and graveyard of the Mount Olivet Baptist Chapel. Looking back from here, it will be appreciated that the Calder Valley must have been very attractive before being sacrificed in the cause of industrial progress, and indeed the hanging woodlands on the steep slopes above the despoiled valley floor still add a certain charm to the scene.

Colden Water

A good path passes behind the ruined chapel, followed by an intricate section of farms, tracks and walls, but the route is more straightforward after crossing a motor road. A rise over a small hill and a descent through pastures leads to the pretty dell of Colden Water and a footbridge, over which there is an ascent to the moorland village of Colden.

Here there is access to the open expanse of Heptonstall Moor and a grooved path across it.

On Heptonstall Moor

The Walshaw Dean Reservoirs in the distance

In bright weather, the crossing of Heptonstall Moor is a very pleasant interlude in the journey. All around is open country, unspoilt and unimpeded by the works of man and with a view forward of rolling hills. Relieving the bleakness of the scene is the richly-wooded valley of Hebden Water on a parallel course down on the right. Further, an area appropriated for the conservation of water is reached, five impounding reservoirs having been constructed here to gather the flow from the surrounding heights. The landscape is desolate and as some lonely waterworks cottages are passed, a memory is revived of the tragic death in a blizzard of the reservoir keeper, with its warning that the moors, even to a man familiar with them, can be extremely hostile in severe weather.

Two footbridges crossing the outflows from the reservoirs point the way to the wild moorland road linking Colne and Hebden Bridge, and here an agonising doubt may arise: whether to go along the road to the right, off route, for half a mile to seek refreshment at the Pack Horse Inn, the name being a reminder of an earlier mode of transport, or to continue steadfastly along the Way. In the latter case, the road to the left must be followed to a locked waterworks gate with a stile to give pedestrian access to a works road formed of two strips of concrete for wheeled traffic with happily a strip of grass between for boots. A dam between the upper Walshaw Dean Reservoir and the lower is crossed and, with a few exotic rhododendrons gracing the scene, the reservoir environs are left behind on a path ascending Wadsworth Moor. On this gentle rise is a boulder with a tablet affixed by the Spen Valley Ramblers in memory of a club member who died on this spot. Higher, looking back, Stoodley Pike can be seen backed by Blackstone Edge, already far distant. Then, on the crest of the moor at Withins Height, the Brontë country is entered.

Top Withens   Below *The plaque on the wall*

On Withins Height, a new and unattractive landscape is revealed ahead, dreary moorlands descending gradually north to the valley of the River Worth. The foreground is harsh and sour, without life and without beauty. But it is rich in literary associations, and excitement mounts for those numbered amongst the countless admirers of the Brontë sisters as a ruined building comes into sight across a neglected pasture. This is Withins, or Top Withins, reputedly the Wuthering Heights of Emily's classic novel.

Withins is a decayed skeleton of a house, with crumbled bones and sightless eyes, perched high on a windswept moor and ravaged by storms; forsaken, abandoned to nature, the field walls broken and the grass grown coarse and rank around it.

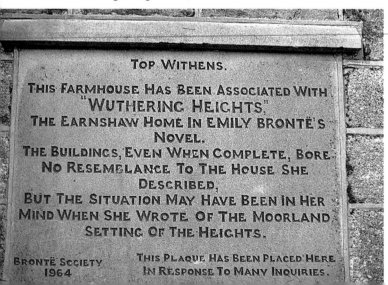

Such is Withins today, in sad plight yet not different from a hundred other ruined farmhouses high on the Pennines. But public imagination, inspired by the novel of Emily Brontë, has long regarded Withins as her Wuthering Heights and the ruin has become a place of pilgrimage. The setting is grim, a lonely dwelling in a wasteland of heather and peat. In its day, Withins must have been a house of good appearance as the dressed stones and mullions and buttresses still testify, but that day has gone. Only the ghosts of the past find shelter here and only the few trees nearby show life.

Ponden Hall

Beyond Withins, the Worth Valley is seen in more detail, and a path, becoming a lane, descends into it through farms to the corner of Ponden Reservoir amongst scenery that is still austere and marred by many derelict buildings. The Way goes left, skirting the reservoir and passing Ponden Hall to reach the Colne–Keighley road.

Ponden Hall deserves more than a passing glance. This seventeenth-century farmhouse is well known and much visited for its Brontë associations, being by repute the Thrushcross Grange of *Wuthering Heights*. It is a building of great character and strong proportions, with much of the original interior happily preserved and featuring wide fireplaces and massive oak rafters. Not less important for Pennine Way walkers, it is one of the few places actually on the route that provides refreshments and accommodation.

At Ponden, the best known of all small Yorkshire towns, Haworth, is conveniently near, two miles from the dam of Ponden Reservoir and reached by road through the village of Stanbury (bus terminus).

Haworth should certainly be visited once in a lifetime. Here is the parsonage for long the home of the Brontë family and now a museum of their effects, the church where they worshipped, and the Black Bull in which Branwell indulged too freely. But, apart from these magnets of public curiosity, the steep main street is of unusual interest and at the bottom of the hill the Worth Valley Railway, operated by amateur enthusiasts, is a great attraction.

Haworth, unfortunately, suffers from tourist invasions. Crowds of sightseers and geriatrics, brought here by coaches, throng the streets, catered for by many shops that seem more concerned with the fancies of visitors than the needs of residents. It is not a place to come to during the day. Only in the early morning or late evening does Haworth fleetingly regain its Victorian charm.

At Haworth : Above *The Parsonage*   Below *The Worth Valley Railway*   Opposite *The main street*

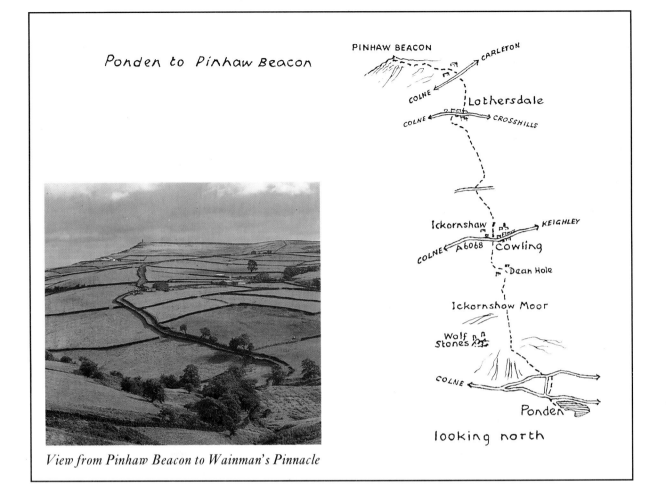

Ponden to Pinhaw Beacon

PINHAW BEACON

CARLETON

COLNE

Lothersdale

COLNE   CROSSHILLS

Ickornshaw   KEIGHLEY

COLNE   A6068   Cowling

Dean Hole

Ickornshaw Moor

Wolf
Stones

COLNE

Ponden

looking north

View from Pinhaw Beacon to Wainman's Pinnacle

THE Colne–Haworth road is crossed at the west end of Ponden Reservoir and a rising path taken alongside the wooded dell of Dean Clough to an upper road (Colne–Keighley), beyond which there is a gradual climb to an open moorland. Wolf Stones, a cluster of rocks with a triangulation column, are seen on the left as the extensive top of Ickornshaw Moor is reached. This is a barren wilderness of tough grass and heather interspersed with peat channels and has a bad reputation amongst walkers. Paths are indistinct or absent and trust must be placed in a line of cairns. The terrain is rough, with ankle-twisting propensities but, compared with the Featherbed Mosses and Black Hills of the Peak District, a children's playground.

This section is unattractive; there is a feeling in the atmosphere that there are industrial towns all around, which is true although none can be seen, and that their dirt and grime has dusted the landscape, an impression emphasised by abandoned and derelict buildings on the descent to the main Colne–Keighley road, the A.6068, passing stacks of peat cut from the moor for fuel. The road is reached at the village of Cowling, not the most salubrious of places, its only claim to fame being that Philip Snowden, the first Labour Chancellor of the Exchequer, was born nearby.

Ruined farmhouses are a sad feature of the Pennine moors. Many of them were originally buildings of substance and character, but with the passing of the years have fallen victims to cruel circumstances. A changed economic climate has brought disaster to the small hill farmer, robbing him of a future.

Victorian gentlemen of the West Riding had a liking for erecting monuments on the hilltops around their homes, mostly in the form of stone towers in a variety of designs and all built by craftsmen, some serving as memorials, some as beacons, some as follies. All survive today as landmarks visible from afar. Modern planning authorities doubtless regard them as desecrations of the landscape, yet permit the television masts, radio booster stations and pylons that disfigure the twentieth-century skylines. The stone towers are an accepted part of the West Yorkshire scene, and respected, but no affection can be felt for the unsightly steel and concrete contraptions of today.

The two towers depicted below stand on Earl Crag, a gritstone escarpment overlooking the Colne–Keighley road, a mile east of Cowling. They are not on the route of the Pennine Way but offer a pleasant evening stroll for anyone staying in the vicinity.

Wainman's Pinnacle   Lund's Tower

From Cowling, the Way passes through the suburbs of Ickornshaw and Middleton, and then follows a 'bitty' two miles of small fields and lanes with many stiles and gates, too intricate to allow attention to be paid to the rural scene, but generally maintaining a northerly direction to the village of Lothersdale. The final approach is along a lane, the village coming into sight suddenly as a picturesque grouping of cottages around a textile mill that is so deep set in its valley that, from this viewpoint, the top of the tall mill chimney is below eye level.

First view of Lothersdale

Lothersdale is a sweet and friendly village, many of the older houses being charming and of a distinctive character. The mill is interesting, Lothersdale Beck flowing in a tunnel beneath and formerly operating a water wheel. The village has long been a centre of Quakerism, the Society of Friends having a meeting house here, and there are literary associations at Stone Gappe, a mansion nearby, featured in *Jane Eyre* as Gateshead Hall. A church, an inn and a shop contribute further to Lothersdale's comfort for Pennine Wayfarers.

Lothersdale

The summit of Pinhaw Beacon

Lothersdale is left with some reluctance by a farm lane and field paths rising to the Colne–Carleton road, which is crossed to pass between farms, the route then turning west to the open moorland of Pinhaw Beacon which, instead of the usual pile of stones expected of a beacon, has only a triangulation column to mark the highest point, this being a grassy mound in a sea of heather.

Pinhaw Beacon, like Blackstone Edge, occupies a key position on the Pennine Way, heralding the beginning of better things to come, a promise that can be anticipated by looking north across the wide valley of the River Aire to the limestone hills around Malham, twelve miles away. Here a new world, a green world, is entered. Considering the modest elevation of the Beacon, 1273 ft, the view is very extensive. Far in the distance are the shapely peaks of Ingleborough and Penyghent, real mountains at last, flanked by the Wharfedale heights. Nearer, south-west, is the whalebacked Pendle Hill, marking the end of industrial Lancashire. It is an exciting prospect. But first the low-lying and entirely pastoral Aire Gap must be crossed, a wide strath devoted to dairy farming. Mud on the boots will henceforth be blended with manure.

All is fair to look upon from Pinhaw Beacon except for one disturbing element: the lines of shooting butts around are sickening reminders of the little game hunters who, from places of concealment and armed with guns, bravely shoot down innocent and defenceless birds, murder masquerading as sport, and enjoy doing so with no feeling of shame. The human animal, supposedly the superior species, is the biggest bully and greatest predator of all.

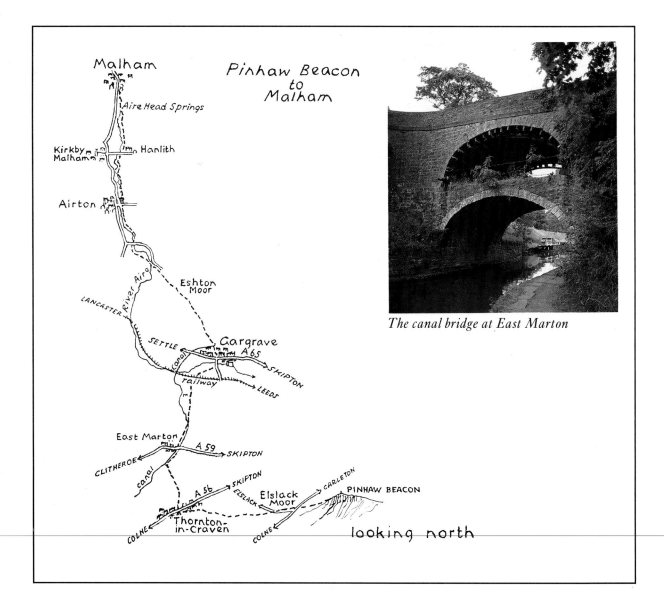

The canal bridge at East Marton

FROM Pinhaw Beacon there is a long but gentle descent amongst the heather of Elslack Moor to the village of Thornton-in-Craven, which contrives to look charming despite the heavy traffic passing through on the A.56, a busy road that also carries the Manchester–Skipton bus service.

A lane continues the Way through a succession of fields, and hereabouts acquaintance is resumed with contented cows. Then the route comes alongside the Leeds and Liverpool Canal, the towpath being followed to the hamlet of East Marton, on another busy road linking Clitheroe and Skipton, the A.59.

The River Aire at Gargrave

I have often been asked to explain the reason why the canal bridge under the A.59 at East Marton has two arches, one above the other, the top one obviously not intended to accommodate the canal. Surely the reason is that the road above originally had a severe dip where it crossed the canal, which didn't matter much in the days of horses and carts but became dangerous with the advent of fast motorised traffic, it then being necessary to raise the surface of the road by about twelve feet. This could only be done by building a superstructure on top of the existing bridge. Solid stonework would have weakened it, the solution adopted being to add another arch, much less weighty but equally as strong as solid stone, as all builders know. That's my theory.

The canal towpath is followed north from East Marton to another bridge, which is crossed to gain access to a complicated series of footpaths with many stiles and gates. As the slight rise of Scaleber Hill is topped, a splendid view of upper Airedale is revealed, and directly ahead is seen the large village of Gargrave, reached after crossing the Lancaster–Leeds railway and passing the church where the funeral service for the politician Iain MacLeod was held a few years ago.

Gargrave is astride an even busier road, the A.65 (Kendal–Keighley) but, away from its noise, the village has quiet byways and spacious public grounds alongside the River Aire. It is the last opportunity for several miles to replenish supplies or obtain overnight accommodation.

Leaving the crossing of roads at Gargrave by the one going north, the canal is met again and here it presents a colourful and animated scene, having been adapted for the mooring of dozens of pleasure boats after its commercial use ended. Over the canal bridge, a lane flanked by trees and plantations heads north-west for Eshton Moor, the lane being succeeded by an indistinct track going in the same direction to come alongside the River Aire. A pleasant walk along its banks upstream arrives at Airton Bridge.

Above *The canal at Gargrave*

Airton Bridge

The 'squatter's cottage', Airton Green

Airton is an attractive village up the hill to the left from the river bridge. There are some houses of distinction, mellowed by age, and many charming old cottages around the village green, in the middle of which, in isolation, is a 'squatter's cottage'. Of special interest is the Friends' Meeting House and graveyard.

The Pennine Way, however, continues along the east bank of the Aire in scenery that becomes very beautiful in the parkland of Hanlith Hall. At the bridge beyond, a visit to the small settlement of Kirkby Malham, the ecclesiastical centre of an extensive parish, should be considered although half a mile off-route. This is a delightful place, the main attraction being the venerable fifteenth-century church with interesting features in its spacious interior and the name of Oliver Cromwell in its registers, he having signed there as a witness to a wedding in 1655. Unlike the better known village of Malham, a mile up the dale and a centre of tourist activity, Kirkby Malham has preserved a sweet seclusion.

Church of St Michael the Archangel, Kirkby Malham

Either side of the Aire may be followed from Hanlith Bridge to Malham, the official route being on the east bank. The west bank is rather more interesting, passing the old manorial mill of Scalegill. This was originally powered by water from the river carried along a mill race still to be seen. On the occasion of my visit, the building was being used as a battery house for hens, and if such use is continuing will be a disturbing sight for those, surely a majority, who feel that all living creatures are entitled to a natural life.

Up-river from here, on the final stage of the approach to Malham, is the first of a series of geological phenomena, the rising of the river from its limestone bed. This place is Aire Head Springs and commonly considered to be the source of the River Aire, although in fact the water appearing here is a resurgence of the stream issuing from Malham Tarn and disappearing at Water Sinks three miles away, having travelled the intervening distance along underground channels. Strange things like this happen in limestone country.

Aire Head Springs

Malham

Now the Way enters Malham, a village small in extent yet known far and wide as a base for the exploration of its fascinating natural surroundings of limestone hills, a wonderland of remarkable rock formations in a landscape of emerald green and dazzling white. Crowds pour into Malham throughout the summer, brought in by cars and coaches, and walkers come here at all seasons of the year. There is a Youth Hostel, an information centre, and private and hotel accommodation. Visitors who come not to walk but merely to potter around the village, find much to interest them and their needs are catered for by shops and cafés. Malham has a charm that draws people not once but often.

Malham is the threshold of the best part of the Pennine Way, the starting point of an exciting journey over limestone uplands of great geological interest. Here in this lovely setting Black Hill and the Featherbed Mosses are like a bad dream. The soggy moorlands are behind and sparkling landscapes ahead. Edale seems a world away. Yet little more than a quarter of the Pennine Way has so far been walked. Those who have not enjoyed the journey thus far will do so from now onwards. Malham is the place where the highlights begin to appear.

BETWEEN Malham and Ribblesdale all is limestone magic, an area of spectacular rocks and caves caused by a major geological fault, and panoramic views of dark moors relieved by many white cliffs and outcrops where the bedrock has broken the surface: a strange landscape, almost lunar, in places awesome, in places beautiful, and everywhere fascinating. A succession of impressive scenes makes this section of the Way a classic walk of sustained interest, a memorable adventure.

The Pennine Way continues due north from Malham, but a visit to Gordale Scar, a long mile to the east, is strongly recommended as a starter to the next stage. The Scar is on the line of the Mid-Craven Fault, where a massive dislocation of the strata has opened a narrow cleft between towering and overhanging cliffs: a scene of majestic grandeur, hidden on the approach and revealed suddenly with dramatic effect. A stream dances down the boulder-strewn ravine, having two waterfalls of which the higher gushes through a hole in the rocks and, after crossing an open pasture, enters a wooded dell. Here, in a sylvan setting, is the charming Janet's Foss.

This detour is a fitting prelude to the day's march.

Janet's Foss   Opposite *Gordale Scar*

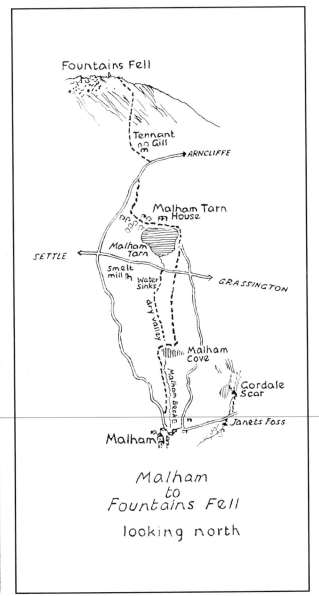

Malham
to
Fountains Fell
looking north

From Malham, the Way resumes its journey north on a much-trodden and tourist-frequented path alongside Malham Beck leading to the tremendous amphitheatre of Malham Cove in view ahead. From the path can be discerned, on the hillside across the stream, the ancient ridged boundaries of Iron Age settlements and a remarkable series of lynchets, the cultivation terraces of the early settlers. But it is the great limestone cliff ahead that most arrests the attention: a sheer wall of vertical and overhanging rock nearly 300 ft high and considered unassailable until post-war cragsmen using pitons and other mechanical aids succeeded in pioneering routes of ascent. The cliff, extending in a long curve, is a majestic and overpowering sight: the greatest natural feature seen on the whole course of the Pennine Way. From an impenetrable cave at the base of the cliff silently emerges a crystal-clear stream, known here as Malham Beck but destined soon to become the River Aire.

Opposite *Malham Cove*
Below *Lynchets near Malham Cove*

Malham Beck

Below *The limestone 'pavement' above Malham Cove*

Escape from the depths of the Cove is made by a steep stairway up the grassy bank to the left of the cliff. On the crest thus attained, another surprise awaits the walker in the form of an extensive platform of naked limestone, a level 'pavement', crisscrossed by a network of narrow fissures and cracks in the sheltered recesses of which flourish small ferns and flowers—a botanist's delight.

This remarkable pavement is traversed to the lowest part of the rim of the cliff, which is seen to be the terminus of a dry valley coming down from the moors beyond. It is a valley with a stream-bed but no stream, carved and eroded by a retreating glacier that, after the Ice Age, carried a watercourse to the lip of the cliff, over which plunged a miniature Niagara. In the course of time, however, the joints in the underlying limestone bedrock were cleared of debris and admitted the water to underground channels. Not for centuries has Malham Cove been graced by a waterfall.

The dry valley

Below *Above Malham Cove*

The top of Malham Cove

The rim of the cliff near the channel of the former waterfall is a splendid vantage point, a place for a leisurely halt and a study of the surroundings. Over the profound abyss of the Cove is a distant prospect of upper Airedale and, nearer, the line of approach with Malham Beck far below. There is an aerial view of the ancient settlements in the fields alongside the stream, more clearly delineated from this lofty perch. All around are escarpments and outcrops, glittering white in sunlight, grey in shadow. But the greatest impact on the beholder is made by the frightening gulf of the Cove, here 240 ft directly below over the abrupt and unprotected edge of the cliff. It is, fortunately, so obviously dangerous that few venture too closely.

This is limestone country at its best, most beautiful and most exciting.

Water Sinks   Below *The old smelt mill*

The official route now makes a beeline for Malham Tarn, due north ahead, but a more interesting approach follows the dry valley upwards to the next notable feature: a slight moorland depression known as Water Sinks, where the stream issuing from the tarn silently disappears underground. The mystery of its subsequent subterranean course is unsolved but the place of its resurgence on the surface has been proved by chemical tests to be at Aire Head Springs, south of Malham village, the uprising being augmented by Malham Beck and the combined waters continuing as the River Aire. The seemingly obvious theory that the vanishing stream at Water Sinks follows the dry valley underground and emerges into daylight at the base of the cliff at Malham Cove has thus been disproved. By similar tests, the stream issuing into the Cove has been found to have its source in waters that sink out of sight on a vast expanse of moorland north-west near the ruins of an old smelt mill, the chimney of which survives and is a conspicuous landmark. Both these underground channels exceed a mile in length, but unlike many of the caves further north, cannot be entered and explored and their exact course remains unknown. At Water Sinks, the stream percolates into its stony bed and vanishes: an odd sight. But walkers in limestone country become accustomed to the unexpected behaviour of its waters and the wayward topography of the area, and they learn much simply by wandering about and looking. At Malham, geology hits you between the eyes.

Malham Tarn

Geography, the lie of the land, is an interest common to all walkers who are usually less concerned with geology, the basic structure of the land, this being an interest acquired only by study and a subject rarely evident visually. North of Malham, however, walkers cannot fail to comprehend the importance of the great geological upheavals of strata that have resulted in the vertical 300-ft cliff towering above Malham Cove and the striking natural features of the terrain beyond. These manifestations are obvious not only to the learned but to all others who enter this enchanted land of delights.

Malham Tarn is another surprise. It is an extensive sheet of water half a mile across and bordered by a fringe of woodland, an unexpected oasis in the midst of bare uplands and over 1200 ft above the sea. 'Tarn' is a misnomer; it would be more properly described as a lake. It is a sanctuary for birds and waterfowl which enjoy here a life free from persecution.

The real surprise, though, is the fact of its existence. It lies in a surround of carboniferous limestone which, being porous and soluble, does not hold surface water but admits it to underground channels and cave systems. Yet here is a large expanse of water open to the sky, discharging only at a normal outlet with a small stream, soon to disappear at Water Sinks. The explanation is geological. The tarn lies on a bed of harder rock, silurian slates, impervious to water and recurring in patches along the line of the North Craven Fault, which influences the landscape hereabouts.

The route joins a carriageway leading to Malham Tarn House, lying amongst trees at the head of the tarn. This section is overlooked by Great Close Scar, a lofty escarpment of fractured limestone crowning a green slope.

Malham Tarn House is a surprise, too. It seems incongruous that such a splendid mansion should ever have been sited in so remote a location in the heart of such a bleak and inhospitable landscape. Originally, the site was occupied by a shooting lodge more appropriate to the surroundings, the present house being built in 1850 as a private residence, and as such it was visited by many literary celebrities, among them Charles Kingsley, whose *Water Babies* was inspired by the scenery. Shorn of some of its ornate features, notably a tower, the property with its extensive grounds is now owned by the National Trust and used as a residential centre by the Council for Promotion of Field Studies. The natural life of the estate is preserved and protected, while the staff caters for groups of students and other interested visitors. The environs of Malham Tarn were formerly unfrequented and little known outside the district, but now on any summer weekend the place attracts many people who are in sympathy with the Council's objects and there is much pedestrian activity on the estate paths, in the woods and on the shore of the tarn, cars happily being prohibited.

Once a shooting lodge for the destruction of birds, now a sanctuary for their preservation: a gleam of hope for the human race too.

The grounds are a nature reserve and bird sanctuary, and the need to prevent disturbance is emphasised by a large number of PLEASE notices: 'keep to the road' . . . 'do not pick flowers' . . . 'shut the gate' . . .'keep your dog on a lead' . . . 'do not leave litter' . . . 'do not move stones' . . . 'no cars' and so on.

Otherwise, you are welcome!

Malham Tarn House

After the excitements of the last few miles, the Way proceeds more sedately through fields until, at Tennant Gill Farm, the ascent of Fountains Fell starts along an old mine track. Here the fresh green of limestone pastures gives way to a much coarser and less attractive ground cover of acid peat and gritstone. There is compensation, however, as height is gained, in the comprehensive views of the distant Yorkshire Dales.

An imperceptible but important watershed is crossed on the short walk from Malham Tarn to Tennant Gill. The gathering grounds of the River Aire are left behind; ahead, along the eastern flank of Fountains Fell, all streams flow to the Wharfe. The Pennine Way impinges only slightly in the drainage area of the Wharfe here, entering Ribble country north of Fountains Fell.

The top of Fountains Fell   Above *Tennant Gill Farm*

Penyghent from Fountains Fell

Fountains Fell takes its name from Fountains Abbey which, in medieval times, was the owner of vast tracts of land in this district. The top is a rough and desolate wasteland of boulders and rocky outcrops, with the works of man evident in a number of stone men (tall cairns), in a small building, shaped like an igloo, that offers the only shelter on the barren summit, and in the shafts of long-abandoned coal mines. The Way does not visit the highest point, at 2191 ft, but slants along the summit plateau to reach its northern edge.

Where the path starts to descend from Fountains Fell, there is a splendid prospect ahead, with Penyghent occupying the centre of the stage. It rises starkly, like the upturned keel of a boat, from a wide plinth of moorland fretted with white outcrops and terraces and pavements that indicate a further acquaintance with limestone. The view also includes Ribblesdale and, more distantly, the lofty background of tomorrow's march. But it is Penyghent, the next objective, that concentrates the attention.

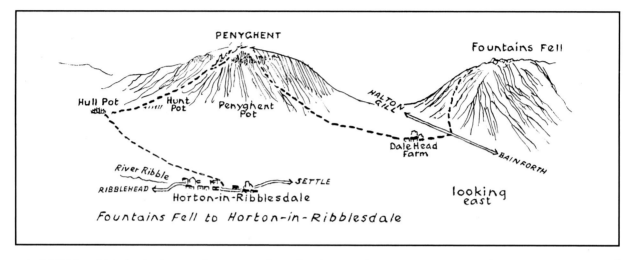

Fountains Fell to Horton-in-Ribblesdale

ALTHOUGH the Ordnance Survey prefer to hyphenate the name PENYGHENT into PEN-Y-GHENT and no doubt have good reason for doing so, hyphens, here as elsewhere, are an irritation, right or wrong, and modern usage omits them. They also prefer to add the suffix HILL, but this detracts from a fine name and is never used in conversation. Walkers speak of PENYGHENT, never of PEN-Y-GHENT HILL.

Penyghent is the highest upthrust of land so far reached on the Way and the first to deserve the name of mountain, having all the characteristics of altitude, steepness of ascent and an airy summit defended by an escarpment of crags. This, at last, is a real mountain. It is an insult to describe it as a hill.

The route to its top follows a wall upwards from Dale Head Farm and rises at a gentle gradient until the escarpment is reached. Here it will be seen that a cap of gritstone is superimposed on the limestone cliff, this darker upper tier being a resort of rock-climbers. This double barrier is surmounted by a stony gully, above which is the broad grassy summit crowned by a large cairn.

The view in all directions is comprehensive. Penyghent, 2273 ft, is one of a trinity of proud mountains known as the Three Peaks, Ingleborough, 2373 ft and Whernside, 2414 ft, being the others—both are prominent in the view across Ribblesdale. These three mountains are of challenging appearance and together form the objectives of Three Peaks marathons for walkers, runners and cyclists: a severe test of stamina and endurance over twenty rough miles of ups and downs.

The view north-west from Penyghent

Penyghent from Dale Head Farm

Below *The summit cairn of Penyghent*

Saxifraga oppositifolia
Opposite *Limestone cliffs, Penyghent*

Hunt Pot

The path of descent from Penyghent's summit first follows the rim of the escarpment northwards until an obvious breach offers an easy route down to the peaty moor below. At the level of the base of the cliffs, a recommended short detour to the right brings into view a remarkable detached pinnacle of limestone 60 ft high, not seen from the path and not generally known. But the secret joy of Penyghent is the adjacent cliff itself and the vegetation that grows there.

Visitors to Penyghent in the month of April will ever afterwards remember it as the mountain of the purple saxifrage, for this beautiful plant decorates the white limestone cliffs on the 1900-ft contour with vivid splashes of rich colour. It is especially rampant along the western escarpment which it drapes like aubretia on a garden wall.

At the base of the western slope of Penyghent, around the 1350-ft contour, limestone reasserts itself on the surface with a graphic and exciting exhibition of the effect of water seepage on soluble rock over ages of time. Here is a series of caves and potholes providing underground adventure for speleologists. Some are no more than narrow fissures, some descend from sinkholes in the moor, and a few are open to the sky, their dangers patently obvious.

Of these subterranean cave systems, the greatest is Penyghent Pot, entered by a small and seemingly insignificant aperture that gives access to a labyrinth of low waterworn passages and a succession of potholes penetrating the moor to a depth of over 500 ft: it is an extremely arduous and dangerous descent with a record of casualties. Penyghent Pot is half a mile off-route and its unspectacular entrance is not easy to locate. A search for it is not recommended for tired limbs pursuing the Pennine Way.

Two others should certainly be visited although a little off the line of the path. Hunt Pot is reached by a short detour to the left and identified by a surrounding fence. Here, in a sinkhole, a small stream plunges into an evil slit, at the bottom of which difficult progress is possible to a depth of 200 ft until a choke of boulders bars further exploration.

But the most impressive is Hull Pot, in a shallow valley to the right. This, in contrast, forms a large open crater; it is the largest natural hole in the country, measuring 300 ft in length and 60 ft in width and, being fully illuminated by daylight, of more benign appearance. A stream approaches from the north-east and in times of spate plunges over the lip in a fine waterfall but normally sinks into its bed before reaching the crater to reappear in the intricate depths.

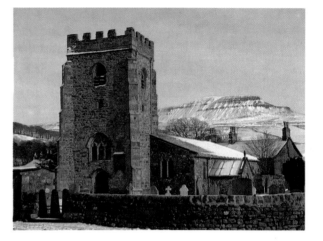

The streams from Hunt Pot and Hull Pot return to daylight near Horton, issuing from separate caves and, curiously, having crossed during their journeys underground.

The day's march ends with a descent to Horton-in-Ribblesdale along a 'green road', typical of many in the limestone areas of the northern counties: a delightful grassy track between white walls. Horton-in-Ribblesdale is a straggling village with hotels and private accommodation and a popular café. There is a Youth Hostel at Stainforth, three miles south along the road to Settle.

Opposite *Hull Pot*   Above *Horton Church and Penyghent*   Below *The green road to Horton-in-Ribblesdale*

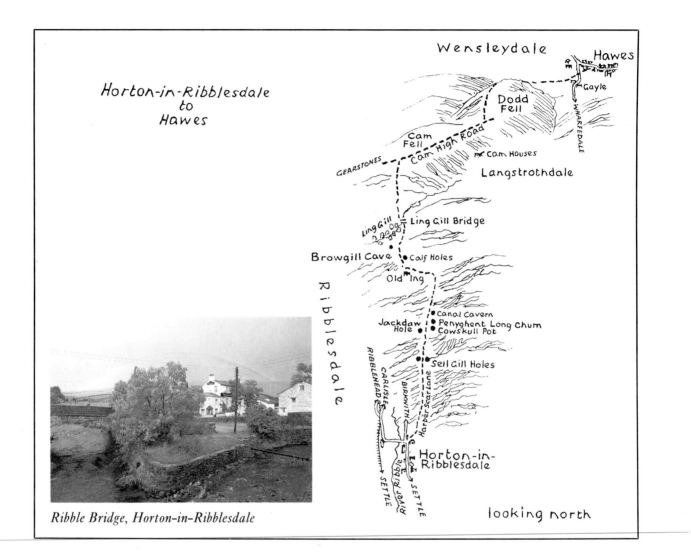

Horton-in-Ribblesdale
to
Hawes

Ribble Bridge, Horton-in-Ribblesdale

FOR fifteen miles after leaving Horton-in-Ribblesdale, there is no hope of obtaining refreshments or lodgings; supplies should therefore be replenished here if necessary and the remaining hours of daylight borne in mind. The village is left by Harber Scar Lane, starting alongside the Crown Hotel and continuing on a rising course between walls for a long mile to Sell Gill Holes, a surprising sight that stops every walker in his tracks. It is the first of a wonderful series of caves and potholes to be seen in the next few miles.

Opposite *Sell Gill Holes*

Sell Gill Holes are limestone formations appearing on both sides of the lane which crosses between them on a natural bridge. On the east side, a stream coming down from the moor is engulfed by a cave and passes under the lane in a subterranean channel to plunge vertically on the west side into a huge cavern 210 ft below ground level. This is the second largest underground hole in the country, Gaping Gill on Ingleborough having pride of place. Exploration of the surface rocks is dangerous. Expert potholers with suitable equipment can descend into the black depths, but others who are absolutely determined to complete the Pennine Way come hell or high water should be content merely to stand and stare.

Beyond Sell Gill Holes, a line of shakeholes, depressions in the ground, will be noticed near the track and parallel to it. These occur where the limestone bedrock has collapsed and probably indicate the presence of underground passages beneath. Then further, over the wall to the left, Jackdaw Hole is seen, a fearful chasm fringed by trees, its perils obvious. A short distance beyond, on the east side of the track, two shafts pierce the moor close together: these are Cowskull Pot, 70 ft deep, and Penyghent Long Churn, 180 ft deep and easily identified by the waterfall pouring into it. These open shafts are unfenced and care should be taken not to frighten sheep grazing in their vicinity.

Canal Cavern is next, passed immediately alongside the track, and a mile further the route turns sharply west, crossing pastures to Old Ing Farm and more excitement.

Jackdaw Hole

___

Old Ing is a lonely farm on a limestone shelf at an altitude of 1200 ft overlooking upper Ribblesdale, with Ingleborough dominant across the valley. It is in the middle of a fascinating network of cave systems with a maze of long underground passages penetrable only by experienced speleologists, although the surface entrances may all be visited by non-experts. This is a wonderful area where I have spent many intriguing hours searching for and locating the many apertures in the moors; but this is a time-consuming pastime with temptations to linger, and walkers bound for the Scottish border should really be away.

Calf Holes

At Old Ing, another lane (the old packhorse road between Settle and Hawes) is joined and heads north, soon reaching Dry Laithe Cave, commonly known as Calf Holes, a spectacular formation where a stream disappears into a cavernous opening in the limestone rocks. This has become a popular picnic spot since motorists discovered that the tarmac road from Horton to Birkwith Farm had been extended to Old Ing. But the real fascinations of Calf Holes are reserved for equipped potholers who can accompany the stream along 500 yards of underground passages to its emergence into daylight at Browgill Cave.

Time is always pressing on the Pennine Way but if half an hour can be spared, it can profitably be spent on a short detour to Browgill Cave, not seen from the lane but reached down a field from a gate near a barn on the left further along. Browgill Cave is a typical cave of debouchure, the stream emerging from a roomy passage after its journey from Calf Holes, and can be entered and followed for 70 yards with the help of a torch until the roof descends to bar further progress except by crawling. Care is needed in walking over the spiky rocks forming the floor of the cave.

Near Browgill Cave is a lime kiln in good condition despite a century of disuse. There are hundreds of such kilns in the limestone areas of northern England, all built to the same pattern with a hearth for burning the stone to produce lime for sweetening the pastures. All are now defunct, casualties of modern methods of mass production—agricultural lime now comes in bags. Much less trouble!

The entrance to Browgill Cave

Ling Gill

Below *Ling Gill Bridge*

The lane continues pleasantly and comes alongside the tremendous ravine of Ling Gill, glimpsed through a fringe of trees. Vertical rock walls and a floor piled high with boulders suggest that this awesome gorge may have been a huge cave, the roof of which has collapsed.

The stream descending into the ravine is crossed by Ling Gill Bridge, a sixteenth-century relic of packhorse days built of gritstone from the bed of Cam Beck. Affixed is a tablet referring to its repair in 1765 'at the charge of the whole West Riding'.

Ling Gill Bridge marks a pronounced transition from limestone to peaty moorland, from a bright landscape to a drab one. Over the bridge, the track starts a gradual climb to Cam End over ground that is juicy underfoot and in places badly waterlogged. Boots get mucky again along here but not as filthy and disgusting as they were on Black Hill nor are conditions as abysmal. Spirits rise, however, as height is gained and distant views open on both sides. In the west appears the threatened railway viaduct at Ribblehead on the Settle–Carlisle line, with Ingleborough and Whernside filling the background, and eastwards there is a prospect over a dreary depression that widens into Langstrothdale.

At a tall cairn on Cam End the Roman road linking Ingleton and Bainbridge is joined, the next section being named Cam High Road in packhorse days. This is followed north-east for two and a half miles on a level track so distinct that it is impossible to go astray and provides dry and very easy walking. But weather conditions at this exposed altitude, around 1700 ft, can be fierce. I have never been so cold as on one winter's day when walking along here in the teeth of a freezing easterly gale, becoming so debilitated by the piercing wind that I began to fear that certain organs of the body necessary for a full life had perished in the blast, a circumstance from which, happily, they recovered and resumed their functions after a rapid retreat to Ribblehead.

Cairn on Cam End

Cam High Road   Opposite *Limestone outcrops along the Cam High Road*

It is interesting to look down from Cam High Road into the depression on the right at the point where the lonely outpost of Cam Houses appears below and note the watershed there. Within a matter of yards, streams form to flow east to the River Wharfe and west to join the River Ribble, the county boundary passing between.

The track continues straight as an arrow after the fashion of Roman roads and unexpectedly becomes tarred, having been adapted as an access to Cam Houses from the Hawes–Kettlewell road further ahead. Hereabouts, the route is on another watershed, the Snaizeholme valley opening on the left and carrying a tributary of the River Ure in Wensleydale and the southern slopes being gathering grounds of the Wharfe. A prominent mortared cairn is soon reached, this marking the point where the packhorse road branches left from the Roman road, and here, if the day be clear, a pause should be made to admire a comprehensive panorama: Penyghent, Ingleborough, Whernside, Wildboar Fell, Buckden Pike and Great Shunner Fell all appearing in a grand circle of uplands. The Way then follows the packhorse road along the flanks of Dodd Fell, now having the name of West Cam Road.

Langstrathdale

Gayle   *Market day, Hawes*

The packhorse road is delightful, being a wide grassy track giving an exhilarating high-level walk along the side of Dodd Fell, shakeholes and limestone outcrops again occurring alongside as the Snaizeholme valley deepens below on the left. When Dodd Fell starts to decline a cairn marks a bifurcation of paths, the one branching to the right being followed over Ten End where there are ancient rights of peat cutting, and then, guided by stiles and gates and with a splendid view of Wensleydale ahead, the Way makes a descending beeline through pastures to enter the village of Gayle. This is a quaint and picturesque settlement of Celtic origin, its great attraction being Duerley Beck which flows in cascades over a limestone bed between groups of old stone houses of individual character. The village is well known for its export of Wensleydale cheese made at a nearby creamery.

Down the road from Gayle a flagged path cuts through fields to enter the main street of Hawes near the church. With the first hundred miles of the Pennine Way now completed walkers who feel that they have earned a mild celebration will find all their needs catered for in Hawes.

Hawes is a small and compact market town, the 'capital' of upper Wensleydale and an important centre of the trade and commerce of the region: an urban community with strong rural interests. The main street is a scene of animated activity especially on market days when crowded stalls add to the congestion, traffic often being brought to a standstill. What a contrast to the profound silence of Cam Fell! There is a Youth Hostel here, ample overnight lodgings, a wide range of shops and forms of refreshment, while those whose celebrations take the form of a pub crawl will suffer paroxysms of delight, several inns lining the street cheek by jowl.

Hawes is an opportunity for licking wounds, enjoying rest and relaxation, and refuelling energy and supplies for the hard days that lie ahead over the next hundred miles.

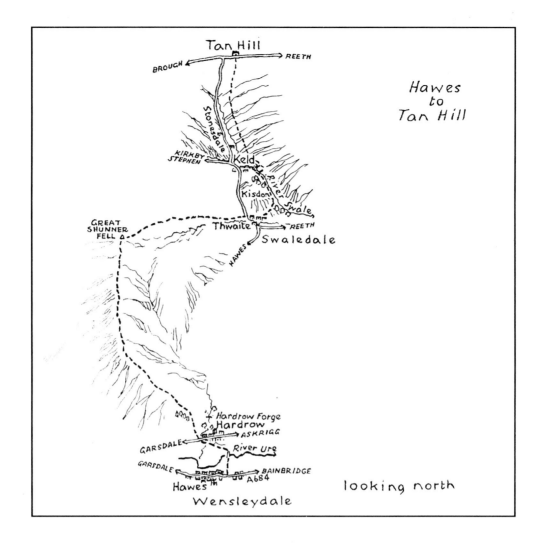

Hawes
to
Tan Hill

looking north

ONE leaves Hawes from the east end of the town near the defunct railway station by a bridge over the River Ure which, although having travelled only a few miles from its place of birth, is already a river in appearance as well as name. Beyond, paths lead to the cluster of stone buildings at Hardrow.

An off-route detour to Hardrow Force should certainly be made. Plunging over a limestone cliff in a single leap of 96 ft, this is the highest surface waterfall in the country (some underground falls are higher, notably Gaping Gill). It is a wonderful sight in a truly magnificent setting at the end of a tremendous ravine enclosed by sheer walls of rock : a savage scene softened by clinging trees.

Hardrow Force attracts crowds of visitors. Access to it is through the door of the Green Dragon Inn, where a charge is made for admission.

The path to the Force has a surprising and unexpected feature. At the entrance to the ravine is a primitive open-air bandstand with terraced seats for patrons, and it is good to know that concerts here have recently been revived. This vast auditorium has a good reputation for its acoustic values, and band contests were regularly held here in happier times gone by. Today's visitors provide their own music of sorts—transistor radios, alas.

Opposite *Hardrow Force*

The route is resumed over the road bridge at Hardrow where a walled lane points the way to Great Shunner Fell, an expansive upland wilderness, twenty square miles in extent, on which clear visibility is a decided advantage. This sprawling mass of high ground should not be underestimated. From Hardrow to the summit the distance is five miles, and they are long miles. At the last wall the path turns away left to the Cotterdale coal pit, long disused, and from here onwards all is open country, a thin track curving up the south ridge of the fell and being generally easy to follow with assurance provided by cairns. On a fine day the long gradual ascent is quite pleasant, far-reaching views compensating for the lack of interesting features nearby. On the ground grassy carpets alternate with rushes, heather and mosses, interspersed with peat hags, pools, shakeholes and rocky outcrops. Man-made contributions to the scene include a sheepfold, a disused quarry, old coal pits, fence posts, cairns and a tall and well-built beacon at Crag End that one hopes will be the summit but isn't. The miles seem endless, but finally, much later in the day, the path trends to the right over rougher ground and there, sure enough, is the cairn and Ordnance column that mark the summit of Great Shunner Fell at 2340 ft, the highest point yet reached on the Pennine Way.

Crag End Beacon

On Great Shunner Fell

The top of Great Shunner Fell is the highest ground on the same latitude between the west coast and the east coast but is not situated on the main watershed as would be expected, this being a few miles west on Abbotside Common where the west-flowing Eden and the east-flowing Ure have their sources. It forms, however, the watershed between the two Yorkshire rivers of Swale and Ure although, curiously, it gives birth to neither.

It is as a viewpoint that Great Shunner Fell excels, the panorama being widespread in all directions. There is a charming view of Swaledale but mainly the prospect is of wild rolling moorlands stretching far into the distance, relieved by the sharper outlines of the magnificent twins of Ribblesdale: Penyghent of recent memory and Ingleborough. The outstanding glory of the view, however, is the western horizon formed by the serrated range of peaks in the Lake District, tremendously exciting even from afar.

A further notable feature of the fell is a series of beacons, all soundly constructed of stone; two are met on the journey, others seen at a distance.

The summit of Great Shunner Fell
Path from Great Shunner Fell

The descent from the summit of Great Shunner Fell to the next objective, the small village of Thwaite, is also long and time-consuming. Initially, the departing path falters but becomes more distinct when a prominent beacon on the north-east shoulder of the fell is reached, thence continuing down to the valley below amongst peat hags. On this descent, lovely views of Swaledale unfold, Thwaite and the next village of Muker coming into sight. The sheet of water seen due north is Birkdale Tarn, originally artificially created to impound water for the smelting mills when lead mining was a considerable activity in the area. But most attention will be directed to the next stage of the Pennine Way, pinpointed by the white speck of the Tan Hill Inn, with the hills of Teesdale beyond. Cross Fell, the highest of the Pennines and on the course of the Way, beckons through the haze of distance.

Gradually the path swings eastwards in a wide arc, passing some trial levels that proved abortive and entering a walled lane that leads directly down to Thwaite where, if luck is in, refreshments can be obtained. Here were born the famous naturalists, the brothers Richard and Cherry Kearton.

Thwaite

Swaledale, at Kisdon

The hill rising behind Thwaite is Kisdon (wrongly spelt Kidson on Ordnance maps—a rare aberration) and from the village the Way climbs to Kisdon Farm and then contours the eastern slope of the hill with the River Swale rushing below between wooded banks. This is the most beautiful section so far, everything being in harmony and making a scene of great charm and loveliness. After two delightful miles the village of Keld is entered almost with regret. If only the whole of the Pennine Way were as pleasant as this!

Once seen and its river environs explored, Keld is never forgotten. Its attractions are unique. This is the last village in Swaledale (or, more properly, the first) and marks a profound transformation in the landscape, a sudden transition from sylvan beauty to barren moorland wildernesses. The little huddle of stone buildings are haphazardly yet tidily arranged on a headland above the River Swale. Little has changed here for generations past, and proud dates and the names of proud men adorn the doorways and walls and even the chapel belfry. A large sundial records the hours, but time here is measured in centuries.

A feature of the background to the village is the large number of isolated stone barns in the hillside fields, standing stark and exposed in a network of limestone walls.

But the joy of Keld is the swift-flowing Swale, embowered in trees, sheltered by white cliffs and broken by falls and cataracts on its wild race from the bleak moors around its sources. At Keld, there is always the sound of the river.

Keld

Opposite *The Keld landscape*

Keld has a Youth Hostel, an austere building that was formerly a shooting lodge, and limited private accommodation for visitors; but the Cathole Inn, once renowned for hospitality, is no more. There is also a chapel, catering both for the living and the dead, and traces of an old Corpse Road along which the fatal casualties of Keld were conveyed by sledge to the nearest consecrated ground at Grinton Church, twelve miles down the valley.

For so small a village Keld has a long history. Its roots are a thousand years old.

The first settlers in upper Swaledale were Scandinavian in origin, and the names they gave to their surroundings have been retained: Keld, meaning 'a place by the river' and Thwaite, 'a clearing', are pure Norse, as are fell, gill, scar, foss and garth.

A later and larger group of settlers in the district were lead miners, working on the hills east of Keld and creating an industry that prospered exceedingly until the turn of this century, when cheaper supplies were obtainable from abroad. All the mines have now ceased to operate, leaving ruins and roofless buildings as sad reminders of an industry that died.

Sundial at Keld

The Keld waterfalls: Above *Catrake Force*
Left *Wain Wath Force* Below *Kisdon Force*

One leaves Keld by crossing a footbridge over the Swale, a path then climbing past East Gill Force to a farm and continuing to rise along a hillside. As height is gained, the view in retrospect is very beautiful, the river curving out of sight along its wooded valley and Keld now being seen perched on a green promontory. This is a scene to be savoured because nothing so lovely will appear again for many a long mile. Indeed, the prospect ahead is dreary in the extreme.

East Gill Force

Swaledale at Keld

The path heads north into a harsh wasteland, being defined by the tracks of farm tractors and, after rain, by ribbons of water. I once walked along this path on the wettest day I can remember, in a sluicing downpour that never relented for an instant. When I left Keld with a lady companion (!) it was already raining hard, but hope springs eternal in a fellwalker's breast and off we went although long experience of wet days should have warned me that the weather would not clear, which it didn't. We arrived after a miserable eternity at the Tan Hill Inn, soaked and squirting water, to find the door locked and no sign of life. We returned to Keld down the road in company with many baby rivers. This was the only occasion in a long career of walking that I sought refuge under an umbrella, and a lady's at that. Afterwards, I did the only honourable thing and married her.

Across Stonesdale, the slender road to Tan Hill can be seen ascending on a parallel course, and on the squelchier parts of the path there is a feeling of envy for the cars speeding effortlessly to the same destination. After fording Lad Gill, an indistinct section indicated by cairns climbs to join an old grass-grown mine road, and the walking then being much pleasanter. Hereabouts, there are open mine shafts, derelict and abandoned, their protective fences having succumbed to old age and the weather: these are in a state of crumbling decay and should not be approached too closely. This is not a path to use after dark.

At last, after topping a rise, the Tan Hill Inn comes into view ahead, a lonely and isolated outpost and seemingly the only building in the world, gleaming like a beacon of hope on the top of sombre moorlands without a vestige of beauty anywhere. The sight is greeted with a muted cheer and steps quicken as the mine road leads unerringly to it.

Approach to Tan Hill Inn

Tan Hill Inn stands at 1732 ft above sea level and is indisputably the highest licenced house in the country. It is of spartan appearance, lacking any pretensions to architectural distinction, its sturdy walls being built to withstand the winds that sweep across the moors and to defy winter storms. It dates back to the early days of coal mining in the area, being erected to serve the thirsts of the miners who worked the shallow seams nearby, producing coal of inferior quality. The inn provided indoor comfort for the men who lived in crude shelters at the work-ings, catering also for the carters who collected the coal, for the travelling tinkers and pedlars who passed this way, and for the drovers who walked their sheep and cattle across these exposed heights to markets in the valleys. These visitors dwindled to nothing, and when I got a night's lodgings here a long time ago, before the war, finding the place rough and primitive but satisfying my needs, I was the first person the occupants had seen for many days.

But today the inn, although not changed in appearance, has a new life and a new clientele. There is affluence here where there was none before. The coming of the motorcar has wrought a transformation in the inn's fortunes. The place has been discovered. It is not unusual on any bright summer's day to find dozens of cars parked on the verges while their owners imbibe inside. And few of the thousands of Pennine Way walkers who arrive every year at this point pass without calling. Things at Tan Hill are not as they used to be.

Before continuing from Tan Hill, the rocky promontory behind the inn repays a visit. Here is the inn's private coal mine and a tablet commemorating an earlier occupant, but the purpose of the visit is to survey the new realms of territory that lie ahead. From this viewpoint, the landscapes are far reaching and distant. Long and uninteresting slopes fall gradually to the wide expanses of Stainmore Forest, not a forest of trees but of vast empty spaces devoid of detail and landmarks. Across a shallow depression, the busy A.66 highway from Scotch Corner to the west coast can be discerned by its moving traffic although yet miles away. This notorious road, passing through the 'Stainmore Gap' at an elevation exceed-ing 1400 ft, is always an early casualty of winter snowfalls. Beyond it are rolling and indefinite moors screening the valley of Baldersdale, and further still the great mass of Mickle Fell fills the horizon. North-east, there is promise of a richer terrain around the village of Bowes which can be seen, its castle prominent, seven miles away, and in the dim distance no more than a suggestion, as yet, of the glories of Teesdale soon to be enjoyed. The prospect pleases.

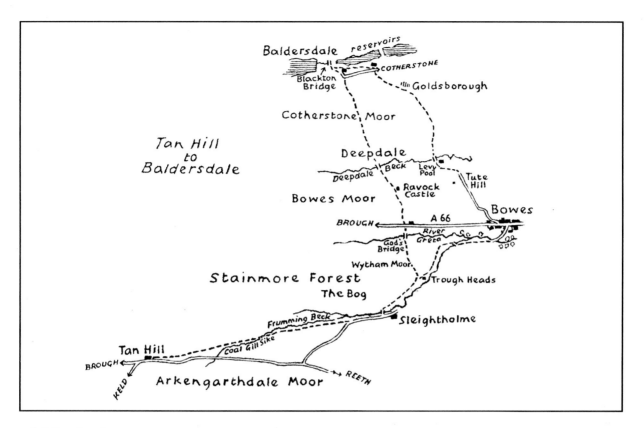

ALTHOUGH the prospect pleases, the first few miles after departing from Tan Hill will not. Walkers who have studied their maps in advance will have noted with apprehension an area named The Bog near the first objective, the farm of Sleightholme four miles ahead. Indicating the likelihood of meeting wet or juicy ground, this is a fear that is soon borne out as conditions underfoot develop the consistency of porridge. The path, which leaves the Reeth road just east of the inn, has the one merit of directness and, having a stream alongside most of the way, poses no problems of route-finding. Cameras can be stored away in the rucksack: nothing worthy of a photograph is seen. The only landmark that catches the eye is Bowes Castle, many miles ahead and not seeming to get any nearer. A little mild interest is generated by the oxbows and gravel beds of Frumming Beck alongside, somewhat relieving the monotony of the journey. But all else is deadly dull.

In due, or overdue, course the path joins the tarmac of the Sleightholme Moor road coming down from the Reeth road. Walkers of low cunning will have noticed on their maps that the squelchy path by Frumming Beck can be avoided, and the whole journey from Tan Hill to Sleightholme and indeed on to Bowes done dryshod, by following the Reeth road to its junction with the Sleightholme Moor Road and turning down the latter, but this is cheating and although nobody will ever know of this defection, it could remain a nagger of conscience.

The road is unenclosed when reached but soon passes between walls to enter the oasis of Sleightholme, a welcome sight.

At Sleightholme, the stream, now called Sleightholme Beck after receiving sundry feeders, is crossed and a path taken to the next farm, Trough Heads. At this point an official alternative known as the Bowes Loop takes a roundabout course to visit the village of Bowes, rejoining the main route in Baldersdale. This narrative will continue along the main route to Baldersdale and then return to Trough Heads to describe the Bowes Loop.

Sleightholme

God's Bridge

From Trough Heads, the main route strikes across Wycham Moor and then, with limestone again in evidence in the landscape, descends to the valley of the River Greta, the principal watercourse of Stainmore, on its way to join the River Tees.

At the crossing of the river, cameras are produced by all who carry them, for here is a remarkable sight, a limestone arch spanning the river bed and of sufficient strength and width to carry an old drove road over it. This natural arch is God's Bridge, one of many so named in the limestone areas of the northern counties and the best example of all. This narrow intrusion of limestone in the native millstone grit of Stainmore has all the characteristics peculiar to it, the river flowing underground in places below a dry and stony bed. Beneath the bridge is a dark deep pool fed by seepage through crevices in the rock walls and is a permanent feature of this spectacular scene.

Ravock Castle

There is a short climb from God's Bridge to an abandoned railway that in its heyday carried trains across Stainmore on a scenic journey between Kirkby Stephen and Barnard Castle. It had the reputation of providing the finest view from any railway in the country: that of the Eden Valley from Barras Station at an elevation of 1300 ft; the railway was the highest in England. These distinctions counted for nothing in the post-war closures of uneconomic railways: the line had the one defect of not paying for its keep and that was enough to seal its fate.

The A.66 is then reached. This important highway runs straight through the Stainmore Gap, or Pass, adopting the course of earlier roads that date from prehistoric times and have long provided a line of communication and trade across the Pennines. It is known that the route was in use in the Early Bronze Age, around 1600 BC, several artifacts and burial mounds of the period having been found, and it seems likely that, even further back in time, nomadic tribes would pass this way. The Romans improved the road during their occupation of northern England, using it as a vital military link between their forts at Brough and Bowes, adding an intermediate camp near the summit of the Pass and fortifying the route by armed outposts and signal stations spaced at intervals, the evidence being plain to see today. Later the road was for many years the scene of battles and border disputes, a relic of those unsettled times being preserved within a railing by the roadside near the county boundary: this is Rey Cross, probably erected about AD 946; its inscriptions have been obliterated by the weather, and only the base of the shaft has survived the centuries. The Vikings were here, too, leaving place names still in use; the Normans, also, who built castles at Brough and Bowes.

Rey Cross

Travellers crossing the Pass in medieval times were often in trouble in bad weather, and shelter and succour were obtainable at a roadside hospital administered by nuns. This was a casualty of Henry VIII's campaign against the monasteries, but a few buildings along the road incorporate the word 'Spital' in their house names.

Deepdale Beck

In historical significance, the Stainmore road is the most important crossed by the Pennine Way.

On arrival at the A.66, it is well to pause on the verge, not only to reflect on the events the road has witnessed through the centuries and to exercise the imagination thereon, but also to ensure a safe crossing to a footpath on the other side. Traffic belts along here at great speeds and any approaching vehicle within 200 yards should be given right of way and no argument. It would be such a pity, and so frustrating after all the effort and suffering of the past few days, and with almost half the journey completed, to have to be taken to a hospital or a mortuary.

Those who survive the hazards of the A.66 next face a gentle ascent on an indistinct track to the crest of Bowes Moor, a good viewpoint for surveying the vast wasteland north of the Stainmore road, in my opinion the greatest wilderness in the country. To the west, as far as the eye can see, are sprawling moors that stretch for many miles to the horizon where Stainmore Common carries the county boundary over ten miles of a wet and mossy plateau and forms the main watershed. This is a no-man's-land, a region that never appears in the headlines nor even in the small print, that is little known and rarely visited even by the fraternity of tough fellwalkers, that has no roads and no paths and no landmarks. The Pennine Way skirts the fringe of this upland desert, and it will be noticed as the walk proceeds that all streams are east-flowing in shallow valleys between low ridges: the terrain, although featureless, has a pattern. These are gathering grounds of the River Tees.

Alongside the track at the top of Bowes Moor is Ravock Castle, an ambitious name for a humble building that at best was merely a shepherd's hut and is today a crumbled ruin.

There is now a view forward of Deepdale, a wide depression along which flows Deepdale Beck, destined to join the Tees at Barnard Castle and already six miles from its source on the watershed at the point where it is crossed by a footbridge after an easy descent from Ravock Castle. In its later stages, this beck flows through verdant woodlands, but here the surroundings are bare and dreary. Few linger by the beck but push on up the facing slope, a straight wall being a sure guide over the next mile to Race Yate on the top of another low ridge.

Race Yate is probably merely the name of the gate that ends the wall and leads onto the open expanse of Cotherstone Moor; apart from a boundary stone, there is nothing of immediate interest. But the height here, 1402 ft, gives the place merit as a viewpoint. Ahead now is the next of the lateral valleys and the greatest, Baldersdale, carrying a watercourse that has carved a deep passage through the moors from its birthplace on Stainmore Common and loses its identity in a succession of reservoirs. Still to the west is the great wilderness, entirely without habitations, but now revealing a notable landmark two miles away in the prominent hill known as Shackleborough, 1489 ft, with a cap of gritstone that has defied erosion. The route now descends gradually but purposefully into Baldersdale, the picture ahead improving with every downward step. Nearing Clova Lodge amongst its welcome trees, the access road to it is met, and at this point the Bowes Loop rejoins the main route.

Here the narrative must halt its progress forward and return to Trough Heads to describe the route of the Bowes Loop.

Baldersdale

The River Greta at Bowes

The Bowes Loop was included in the itinerary of the Pennine Way to give walkers an opportunity of visiting the historically interesting village of Bowes and of securing overnight accommodation and supplies.

Back at Trough Heads, south of the A.66, the Bowes alternative departs from the main route and goes forward by paths and country lanes, passing the confluence of Sleightholme Beck and the River Greta and continuing down the valley in river scenery of increasing loveliness to reach the village, now seen to be dominated by the gaunt walls of the castle.

Six centuries after the Romans abandoned their fort at Bowes, the Normans built a castle on the same site in the form of a massive keep with walls fifty feet high and twelve feet thick. It has long been in a ruinous state following early invasions, but still has a commanding presence, dwarfing neighbouring cottages. It was moated, but the absence of outer defensive walls suggests that its principal use was as a watch tower or garrisoned outpost guarding the Stainmore approach. King John was a distinguished visitor to the castle on two occasions.

Today's visitors are able to call and look round without charge.

Bowes Castle

Dotheboys Hall   Below *Derelict buildings, Tute Hill*

Bowes has a proud literary association. Charles Dickens visited the village in 1838, and in his subsequent *Nicholas Nickleby* gives it the name of Dotheboys, the scene of Mr Wickford Squeers' Academy in Dotheboys Hall and an indictment of the educational establishments of the period. There were four private schools in Bowes at that time, but none with the name adopted by Dickens. Local researchers are of the opinion that his Dotheboys Hall was the large building adjoining the road at the west end of the village. When I was last there Dotheboys Hall had become a transport café.

Bowes is left along a tarred road almost opposite Dotheboys Hall, ascending gradually to Tute Hill and soon having an unsightly derelict area on the left: this is the site of Air Ministry properties, long disused and still displaying notices warning of danger and poison gas.

This is a depressing place. A scene of desolation can be beautiful; a scene of utter devastation is always ugly. Nature fashions desolation; man causes devastation. Nature's wildernesses have charm; man's wildernesses have no charm. The desolation of Stainmore impresses; that of Tute Hill depresses.

Nature creates; man destroys.

The ruins of Levy Pool

The 'Keep Out' signs along the fenced road to Tute Hill seem quite unnecessary: this is the ugliest mile of all and the only concern of walkers is to pass by quickly. At Stony Keld Farm, the tarmac ends and a cart track goes forward to Deepdale Beck, where the ruins of the farm of Levy Pool, or Laverpool, are a sad sight. Presumably a victim of economics, not of the military operations nearby, this must have been a charming complex of buildings before abandonment. The farmhouse, now a gaunt skeleton, still shows character, the barns being thatched, and the whole sheltered by mature trees.

Deepdale Beck is forded and, in unattractive territory, the route crosses a series of undulations formed by four minor ridges with three little east-flowing becks between them. On the right, behind a fence, are announcements, spaced at intervals, proclaiming the presence of an Army Training Area to which visitors are not only unwelcome but exposed to unspecified dangers. As on Tute Hill, the place is a shambles: walls are broken, buildings are ghostly ruins, good earth lies unkempt, any natural beauty that once was there has withered and died. Those who lived here, man and beast, before the military took over, have found pastures new.

The rocks of Goldsborough

After a depressing mile, near more farm ruins, a better prospect is unfolded as the route trends west. Ahead, at last, is something to feast the eyes on: the hill called Goldsborough which, alone amongst these featureless uplands, has a distinctive outline and a cap of gritstone. The path passes below its escarpment, a line of low crags with overhangs that provide such excellent shelter that one feels a little sorry on a fine day not to have cause to take advantage of the hospitality offered.

Beyond Goldsborough, with a comprehensive view of Baldersdale in front, the path descends to the access road to Clova Lodge. Here the official route adds an unnecessary complication, crossing this road to a farm and then proceeding through no less than eight fields to Blackton Bridge. But the Clova Lodge road, followed to the left, is a more direct and trouble-free way to the bridge and saves messing about with a lot of gates and stiles. Whichever alternative is dictated by conscience, here endeth the Bowes Loop, the main route being rejoined before crossing Blackton Bridge. Nearby is a Youth Hostel.

Blackton Bridge, incidentally, is the midway point on the Pennine Way, according to my reckoning. Half has been done and half remains to be done.

The completion of the first half of the Pennine Way calls for a mild celebration, but Baldersdale offers no opportunity for this, there being no place of liquid refreshment within miles. Baldersdale, although carrying a major tributary to the Tees and being much the largest of the lateral valleys draining eastwards, is very quiet, free of tourist traffic, and indeed was hardly known outside the district until the opening of the Pennine Way and later the television appearance of old Hannah, who managed her dairy farm alone and was happy and content to do so despite adversity, giving us all an inspired lesson in independence and courage that ought to have shamed many of society's subsidised groaners. There are a few scattered farms on the hillsides, but no village, no church, no inn, no shop.

Baldersdale, however, was known to the water authorities, who have taken over the valley in a big way, their reservoirs and ancillary works extending for many miles. The Blackton and Hury Reservoirs east of Blackton Bridge have recently been augmented by the huge Baldershead Reservoir higher in the valley: this latest addition has a massive earth dam 3030 ft long and 157 ft high, the largest in the country, impounding four million gallons of water.

Standing on Blackton Bridge, the immensity of these operations can be appreciated. The landscape has been transformed, the new dam dominating the scene, with the River Balder emerging from a tunnel below it. One cannot but feel sorry for the River Balder: once it ran free in a channel of its own choice, but is now captive and its course dictated by man. Once it had flowery banks where there are now concrete walls; it used to have such fun in times of spate but today its flow is controlled in measured gallons per minute, no more, no less. No longer is there joy in being Baldersdale's river.

Baldersdale Waterworks

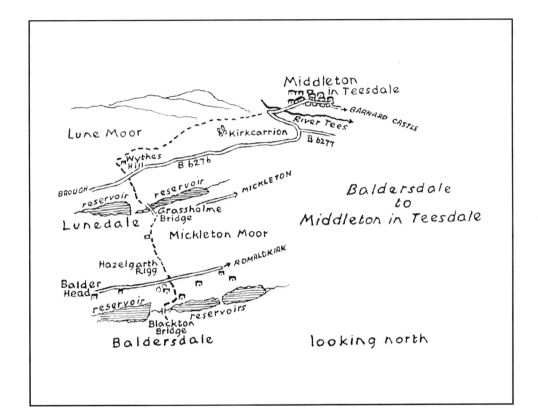

FROM Blackton Bridge, the route passes through gated waterworks property and then paddocks and pleasant pastures, and along lanes to two farms, Birk Hat and High Birk Hat, the latter in particular in a lovely wooded setting.

A quiet country road is crossed, this terminating higher in the valley at Balder Head, the name being an unkind reminder to Pennine Wayfarers who are losing their hair, and a slight ascent made over the uncultivated tract of Hazelgarth Rigg. Strange towers away to the right indicate the line of a two-mile water tunnel linking the Baldersdale and Lunedale reservoirs. A descent follows through farmlands into Lunedale which is almost a replica of Baldersdale: two large reservoirs fill the valley with a road passing between them over Grassholme Bridge.

Beyond Grassholme Bridge, field paths lead up to the Brough–Middleton road, the B.6276, which is crossed to a lane going up to the lonely farm of Wythes Hill. Then follows a confusing mile on an indistinct path through a succession of small fields reaching 1400 ft in altitude to enter a large enclosure. Since leaving Keld, the scenery has been third rate, except for the detour to Bowes, but now it becomes first rate as a glorious view of Teesdale unfolds. To the right is a conspicuous clump of trees surrounded by a wall on a green hill. This is Kirkcarrion, the site of a great tumulus or ancient burial ground believed by the locals to be haunted.

High Birk Hat

Below *Lunedale*

Kirkcarrion

Below *Grassholme Bridge*

Kirkcarrion is a very prominent landmark, its dark cap of trees identifying it from afar, first coming into view at Tan Hill and being glimpsed sporadically as successive low ridges are surmounted, and then remaining in sight throughout mid-Teesdale. It is the forward prospect that compels attention; from Kirkcarrion, the ground falls away sharply into Teesdale and reveals a wide sweep of the valley, all of it beautiful, while for walkers in need of rest and refreshment Middleton, now seen directly ahead and below, is a most welcome sight.

Teesdale from Kirkcarrion

Inspired by the anticipatory delights of Middleton, the grassy descent from Kirkcarrion will be enjoyed, spirits soaring as every step draws nearer to the village and reveals more intimately the loveliness of the valley, with its promise of splendid walking to follow in sylvan surroundings. But it is Middleton that fixes the attention, and when the B.6277 is joined near the disused railway terminus, it is a short road walk over the river bridge to the village. The Pennine Way actually goes upriver from the bridge but few walkers resist the opportunity of visiting the shops and inns and cafés in the streets just beyond. Middleton is not a place to miss.

Middleton in Teesdale as seen on the descent from Kirkcarrion   Below *Middleton Bridge over the Tees*

Middleton in Teesdale, although no more than a large village, is the 'capital' of Upper Teesdale, being the only commercial and shopping centre over a wide area and a convenient base for tourists and walkers. It was at one time the headquarters of a lead mining industry conducted by Quakers who came here in 1815 and operated a flourishing business until its rapid decline at the turn of the present century. During their long period of prosperity, the Quakers developed the village considerably, providing shops and schools and social facilities. They were great benefactors, but the only remaining reminder of their enterprise and generosity and great contribution to the welfare of the community is the clock tower on their former office building.

Middleton has recovered from the loss of its industry and there is a large range of shops and commercial activities, with a choice of hotels and private boarding houses. Bus services and coaches are the only means of public transport since the closing of the railway. The influx of visitors continues to increase as the unique charms of the district become better known, and they are well catered for along the attractive streets. A special feature of the church is the sixteenth-century detached campanile or belltower, a rare architectural curiosity.

The clock tower

The detached bell tower

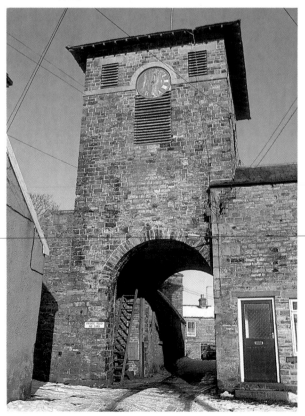

Main street, Middleton in Teesdale

From Middleton onwards, no port of overnight call is met on the route of the Pennine Way until the Eden Valley is reached, and between these two points there are twenty miles of walking, the later stages being across the high moors of the watershed in very wild terrain: an unremitting slog with gritted teeth and little opportunity to rest and enjoy the many natural wonders to be seen along the way.

A much better plan is to break the journey overnight by turning off-route to Langdon Beck, where there is a Youth Hostel, an hotel and limited cottage accommodation that should preferably be reserved in advance of arrival. Such an arrangement would be far more rewarding than a rushed journey, enabling a leisurely approach to be made along Teesdale, which deserves to be savoured slowly. Nothing more scenically beautiful than this part of the valley will be met during the rest of the Way, every step of the eight miles to Langdon Beck being a delight to the eyes and easy on the feet. This section should be walked slowly to gain a full appreciation of the superb river scenery. Eight miles is not much ground to cover between morning and evening but, after all, an easy rest day has been well earned.

And then there are the flowers. Upper Teesdale is known far and wide for its rich botanical displays. In early summer especially there are great drifts of wild flowers augmented by some garden escapes, a kaleidoscope of colour, in enchanting array all along the riverside. The Tees, fringed by trees and copses, is a sparkle of cascades and waterfalls as it rushes down from the hills to reach the placid pastures of Middleton. This is a walk of near perfection.

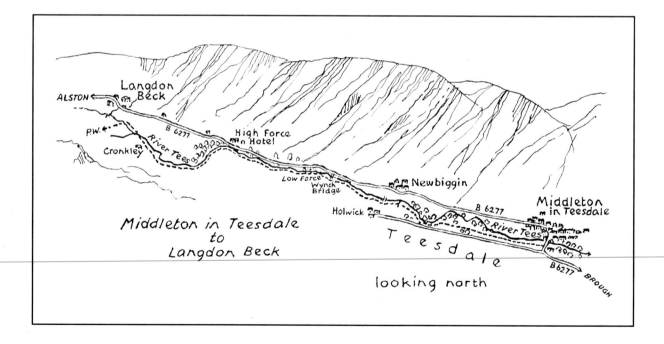

HAVING confirmed that cameras are fully charged, the Way is resumed along a cart track leaving the south side of Middleton Bridge, this soon dwindling to a path as it passes through fragrant meadows and pastures to come alongside wooded dells and banks that give glimpses of the river below.

Right *The River Tees near Middleton*   Overleaf *Summer flowers in Upper Teesdale*

The River Tees forms the county boundary between North Yorkshire and Durham almost throughout its course. The walk is on the Yorkshire bank and there are three opportunities only of crossing the river dryshod to seek the fleshpots of Newbiggin, if any, or of the tourist-infested High Force Hotel on the more hospitable A.6277 running along the Durham bank on a parallel course; on the unpopulated Yorkshire side, there is no sustenance to be found other than grass and rare botanical specimens.

The first opportunity occurs when Scoberry Bridge is reached: this is a footbridge linking the small village of Holwick with the larger community of Newbiggin, one of a dozen Newbiggins in the northern counties, the name meaning 'new building'.

Before leaving Scoberry Bridge, the river bed is worth inspection. Here it is attractively rocky and there are evidences of the force of the swirling waters in the pitted holes in the boulders.

Scoberry Bridge

Holwick

The river scenery continues to be of engrossing interest, apart from its great appeal to botanists, but should not rivet the attention exclusively. Terminating a minor road from Middleton, and worth more than a fleeting glance across the fields to the left, is Holwick, the most northerly village in Yorkshire, its tiny huddle of buildings dwarfed by the long escarpment of Holwick Scar immediately above and exploited by quarrying operations. The Yorkshire side of the Tees rises much more steeply than the moors across the river in Durham, the cliffs recurring often and finally culminating in the great bastion of Cronkley Scar higher in the valley.

A mile further, the river narrows and rushes through rocky channels under a canopy of trees. Here in a picturesque setting is a footbridge out of the ordinary, suspended over the water by two strong chains. This is Wynch Bridge; the original structure erected in 1704 was claimed as the first suspension bridge in England, its purpose being to enable miners to cross the river from their homes in Holwick to the lead mines on the Durham side. After buffeting by floods and a partial collapse, the bridge was restored to its present state in 1830.

Wynch Bridge is a popular venue, attracting visitors from a car park on the B.6277, which here comes alongside the river, their main objective being an open grassy bank nearby, a lovely picnic spot overlooking a delightful display of cascading and splashing waters. This is Low Force.

The Tees at Wynch Bridge   Above *Wynch Bridge*   Opposite *Low Force*

Holwick Head Bridge   Opposite *High Force*

A pleasant walk upriver from Low Force leads to the last of the bridges: a farm access to Holwick Head House from the B.6277. Half a mile distant along the road is the High Force Hotel, surrounded by parked cars and coaches that have brought the multitudes to see the greatest waterfall in the country. Here the queues for refreshments may be joined.

The Pennine Way, however, continues along the Yorkshire bank, high above the river, now in open heathland, the habitat of juniper and, according to warning notices, of adders. The Tees has thus far been a noisy companion, but not obtrusively so, the music of its waters making a harmonious symphony, but gradually there comes an awareness of a dull roar ahead, growing louder, and quite suddenly High Force is revealed. It is a sight that stops every walker in his tracks.

High Force is not the highest waterfall in England, but it is by far the biggest. No other creates such a profound impression on the senses, no other has so dramatic yet beautiful a setting. The thunderous crash of its waters can be heard from afar; they fall without grace in a furious rage. It is a spectacle all should see. A great many do, for this is a showplace of great renown. A convenient hotel and a car park on the B.6277 and a good path (entered upon payment of a toll) winding down through a woodland ensure a crowded patronage on the Durham side of the river.

High Force occurs where the Tees, after a long and restless journey through wild moors from its source on Cross Fell, suddenly plunges over a drop of seventy feet in its rocky bed into a wooded gorge buttressed by huge vertical walls. It is a transition in seconds from one extreme to another. Normally there is one fall only, but after heavy rain it is usual for a supplementary fall to appear, while in times of heavy spate the full width of the gorge can become a tumult of thrashing water. The scene is enhanced by the dolerite formations and by deep pools overhung by foliage.

This is the Tees' finest moment.

Looking down from the top of High Force

Beyond High Force, the landscape changes. Sylvan beauty is left behind and a sterner prospect lies ahead, high and sombre moors crowding into the valley and filling the horizon: this is the area of the Teesdale Nature Reserve. Trees persist across the river and then a large quarry as the path, still amongst rampant juniper, follows a wide curve of the Tees to the isolated farm of Cronkley in austere surroundings. Here the Way uses the farm bridge to cross the river for the first time to the east bank, its final departure from Yorkshire. Then the course of the Tees changes direction sharply, emerging from a defile due west between the heights of Cronkley Scar and Widdybank Fell. Here, at a confluence, the tributary stream of Langdon Beck is followed, leaving the Tees temporarily, and a mile further the B.6277 and the overnight comforts of Langdon Beck are reached.

Thus far the Pennine Way, although occasionally faltering in direction, has contrived to maintain a resolute course northwards with the Scottish border as the target, but at Langdon Beck the route turns not only west but actually trends south of west, the next section ending considerably further from the ultimate objective than it was at the start. Thus far, too, the Way has shown a decided preference for the east side of the Pennines but now crosses the main watershed and descends into the Eden Valley. This is not a day wasted, however, despite the abortive mileage, having two natural wonders deserving of description as highlights and justifying the long detour.

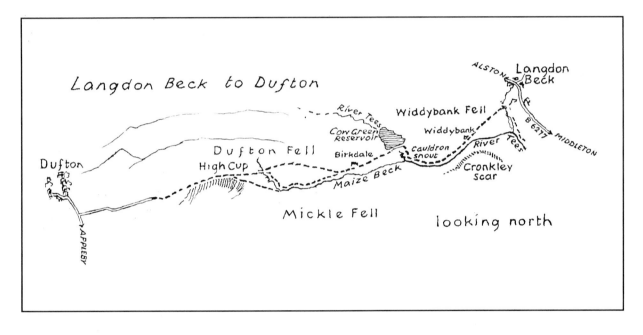

THE Way is resumed by crossing a gated farm bridge over Langdon Beck with good dolerite formations in the stream bed beneath, and then slants across the fellside to rejoin the Tees near Widdybank Farm. The scene here, directly below the cliffs of Cronkley Scar, is very impressive. Nearby are the ruins of a pencil mill, used in the manufacture of slate pencils, the material coming from an intrusion of slate on the fellside. 'Widdy' is a local name for 'pencil'.

Widdybank Farm

*Spring Gentian
(Gentiana verna)*

Widdybank Fell has a unique and well-known attraction that has nothing to do with the making of slate pencils. It is one of the very few habitats of *Gentiana verna*, the beautiful spring gentian, and because of this rare distinction was the centre of a fierce controversy in the 1960s that agitated not only the caring people of Teesdale but interested parties throughout the land and even abroad.

The infant Tees, from its birth on Cross Fell, drains a wide area of rolling moorland that appears at first sight to be a desolate waste, an upland desert of peat and moss and bog and heather, a barren, hopeless wilderness. No region in the country, however, has yielded more valuable secrets to the searchers of scientific truths in those fields of enquiry dear to the naturalist. The geological interest here is great and the fauna is outstandingly rich and varied, but it is the remarkable flora of the district that has most firmly established its place amongst the important regions of natural history in Britain and as one especially worthy of conservation. It is, indeed, an area of international repute and is regularly visited by scientists and students, while a permanent resident team at Moor House conducts continuous research.

This interest is shared by many who, seeking beauty rather than knowledge, simply love to wander in flowery pastures or alongside tumbling waters, and find pleasure in looking for the species of plant life that are rarely seen, not with any thought of pillage but for true enjoyment.

It was against this background of amenity and study and conservation that proposals by the water authorities to establish reservoirs in Upper Teesdale stimulated great opposition from botanists, scientists, outdoor enthusiasts and lovers of Teesdale generally. Most seriously under threat was the shallow basin of the Tees at Cow Green above Cauldron Snout. It was argued that a reservoir here would do grievous and irreparable damage to the cause of conservation by flooding an area of importance to research and by controlling the flow of the river.

Big Brother won in the end, as he usually does, the need for reserves of water for Teesdale being deemed greater than the need to preserve the natural heritage of Teesdale. Parties of volunteers then applied themselves to removing rare species of plants from the valley floor and replanting them above the water line of the new reservoir before the contractors moved in.

Cow Green Reservoir is now established. A battle has been lost, but has a battle been won?

Surely the beautiful Tees, of all northern rivers, was born to run free?

Cronkley Scar

From Widdybank Farm, the path keeps closely to the river, negotiating occasional clusters of boulders and gradually entering an amphitheatre formed by the lofty heights enclosing the narrowing valley: a wild scene emphasised by the rushing river in its stony bed. The most spectacular feature hereabouts is the towering cliff of Cronkley Scar high above.

Falcon Clints   Opposite *Cauldron Snout*

Around a wide loop of the river, the path crosses the debris and scree fallen from the rocky escarpment of Falcon Clints up on the right. All the time, the surroundings become more impressive. Retrospective views are confined by intervening slopes. This is a different world, a world of small compass, its limits the dark moors and only the river showing movement. It is still Teesdale, but the Teesdale of High Force has been left behind. The silence is profound, broken only by the tinkle of the river. There is a feeling, encouraged by a study of the map, that some dramatic scene is not far ahead.

And then suddenly, on rounding a corner, there is the sound of tumbling water and the cascades of Cauldron Snout come into sight, looking at a distance like a torn white ribbon draped down the black rocks of a cliff. But, on closer acquaintance, one finds a turmoil of thrashing spray falling through a height of two hundred feet, its headlong plunge interrupted by rocks and breaking into a series of cataracts.

Cauldron Snout is the Tees in angry mood, and has every reason now to be even angrier since its free flow has been harnessed and controlled by the new Cow Green Reservoir just above. No longer does the Snout reflect the surging torrents coming off the moors in times of spate when the fall was truly spectacular, but one must hope that a sufficient volume of water is released from the reservoir to allow Cauldron Snout to give an effective display and continue to be a delight to visitors.

This is the last section of the Tees to accompany the Pennine Way. Below the Snout is a confluence where Maize Beck joins the river and indicates the further course of the Way, the point of junction also marking the boundaries of three counties.

An exhilarating scramble up the steep dolomite rocks on the east side of Cauldron Snout leads up to a bridge at the top of the cascades. Ahead, the new reservoir is seen, to many people an object of regret and shame. This is the place to say goodbye to the Tees, a spirited companion for many miles but here uncharacteristically a large sheet of unmoving water with all the life and ecstatic exuberance drained from it. A farewell doubly sad.

From the bridge, a farm road heads south-west to Birkdale; this was once regarded as the loneliest of all northern farms but it has had its isolation shattered since the opening of the Pennine Way by thousands of boots pounding past. It remains, however, a very lonely spot, and there is even lonelier territory ahead.

Cow Green Reservoir

Below *Birkdale*

Birkdale is the last outpost of civilisation. Beyond is the main watershed of the Pennines but still four rough miles distant across a wilderness of peat and heather and at an altitude of 2000 ft. On a fine day, the crossing will be enjoyed, conditions underfoot being a good deal pleasanter than they were on Black Hill and the Peak. In bad weather, however, it can be a wearisome trudge with some uncertainty about the line of the route in the absence of landmarks, the comfort of walkers not being helped by a succession of warning notices indicating the limits of a shelled area of the artillery range at Warcop Army Camp seven miles south. The signs warn that 'you pass here at your own risk', but there is no need to run, the boys at Warcop being reliable in their aim.

From Birkdale, Grain Beck is forded and a beeline made for the spoil heap of an old mine, with a crumbled ruin nearby marked on Ordnance maps as Moss Shop, formerly a workshop and living quarters for the miners. Then follows the section that needs clear visibility: the indistinct crossing of a featureless moor with the green grass of limestone making a welcome change as the route descends to come alongside Maize Beck, which incidentally is a safer guide from Birkdale in misty conditions although longer.

Maize Beck

The walk upstream alongside Maize Beck on a limestone bank with many charming features is delightful. After half a mile in its company, large cairns on both sides of the water mark a possible crossing-place. Maize Beck carries a considerable volume of water: it should be forded at this point, unless running high, to a good path on the opposite bank that leads directly across the watershed to High Cup. If, however, the crossing is too difficult, the walk should be continued along the north bank to a footbridge at the head of a spectacular gorge where the limestone rocks, curiously dimpled, nurture many plants, notably the handsome rose-root, in cracks and crevices. With the crossing of the footbridge, the Way passes from east to west of the Pennines and a clear path leads to High Cup—and a sight unforgettable.

High Cup is revealed suddenly, without warning, and the effect is awesome. A profound abyss opens dramatically at one's feet, a massive symmetrical bowl rimmed by a formation of columnar basalt crags that maintains a remarkably level contour all the way round. Below the line of crags, steep slopes of tumbled boulders fall into the depths where a small stream winds westwards to join the River Eden. High Cup is more commonly referred to as High Cup Nick, a name strictly appropriate only to a cleft in the northern escarpment of the vast amphitheatre.

High Cup is a geological phenomenon, a natural wonder.

The path skirts the rim of the northern escarpment of High Cup and a slender pinnacle of rock that has defied erosion in a cleft of the crags is soon seen on the left. This surprising obelisk has the name of Nichol's Chair, or Nichol's Last, after a Dufton cobbler who not only climbed it with the tools of his trade but, so the story goes, soled and heeled a pair of boots while sitting on the top.

The path continues on a high-level course, passing a welcome spring known as Hannah's Well and giving retrospective views of High Cup that illustrate the amazing symmetry of its cliffs.

Opposite *High Cup*   *The cliffs of High Cup*

Dufton

As the path starts to descend from High Cup, a beautiful aerial view of the Eden Valley opens up in front: the fairest panorama yet seen. On both sides, the Pennines drop abruptly to the wide green strath of the River Eden, still far below, their fall being interrupted by a line of steep conical foothills. But it is the prospect ahead that compels attention. Behind now are the restless contours, the dark moors that have formed the landscape since leaving Airedale, and stretching for miles in front are the gentle undulating fields of pastoral Westmorland. Colours are no longer brown but emerald green. The stark upland wildernesses that always seemed to carry a threat have given place suddenly to a quiet, comforting beauty that carries only an air of profound peace. And in the distant background, the most inspiring sight of all: the long serrated skyline of the fells of the Lake District, exciting and beckoning, and surveyed with emotion by those who know and love them. Nothing in the Pennines can offer the exhilaration and romantic charm of Lakeland, and there must be many walkers who, as they come down from High Cup, fervently wish their next steps could be towards the magic mountains seen in the west. But it is not to be. Their present aim is to complete the Pennine Way. The fells of Lakeland will wait.

The path enters a lane that leads unerringly downhill to the lovely village of Dufton, its buildings spaced around an open green edged by mature trees: a pleasant halting place with hospitality and accommodation on offer, including a Youth Hostel that has replaced one at the village of Knock, a mile beyond. Others may prefer to turn off-route to seek the greater facilities of Appleby, three miles away and this must be a definite recommendation for anyone who has never visited this ancient county capital, the most delightful of small northern towns. An overnight stay here, with a leisurely perambulation of the shops and places of historic interest and a return to Dufton the next afternoon, will add a rewarding day to the itinerary.

The ancient borough of Appleby, honoured by a succession of Royal Charters dating from 1179, has an eventful history, recorded from the tenth century when Danish settlers founded a community. Before their coming, but not documented, were occupations by the Celts and the Anglo-Saxons, and the Romans had camps nearby. At the time of the Normans, the area was part of the Scottish Kingdom. Choice of site may have been influenced by considerations of defence, for the town lies within a great loop of the River Eden and is also protected by the hill on which the castle stands. These natural defences were of no avail, however, against raids from over the Border, which ravaged the town in the twelfth century and laid it waste in the fourteenth.

APPLEBY

The Latin inscription on the town's Coat of Arms, translated, is a defiant echo of the past: NEITHER BY FIRE NOR SWORD

Appleby, prior to this latter misfortune, had become a place of great importance, with a population twice that of today, but it never fully recovered its proud status. It suffered further from the plague of 1598 and then defeat in the Civil War when it supported the Royalist cause, and sadly declined in influence although remaining the county town and the centre of traditional ceremonies. The older part of the town has retained its quiet dignity and attractive appearance and escaped disturbance resulting from the coming of the railway and heavy traffic on the A.66. Of its two railway stations, on competing lines, one has gone and the other is under threat. But the Eden flows through as it has always done, and as beautiful as ever, effectively preserving the best of Appleby in a tranquil backwater.

Times have changed again in Appleby. The town has experienced many blows to its pride over the centuries without ever losing it. In 1974, under local government reorganisation, the county of Westmorland was merged in the new county of Cumbria, much against the wishes of most Westmerians, and Appleby lost its long distinction as a county capital, not without protest. Big Brother won again, but Appleby's good folk had the last word, changing the town's name to Appleby-in-Westmorland. Its pride lives on.

Appleby's medieval history is interwoven with the name of the early owners of the castle, the Cliffords, a family distinguished by service to the Crown. The last of the line was Lady Anne Clifford, born at Skipton Castle in 1589. She was a woman of remarkable determination who left an indelible impression on Westmorland affairs by dedicating her life to the restoration of castles and churches and bridges in the north and to the welfare of the people living on her large estates.

Among her many benefactions were the alms-houses founded in 1651 for widows, pleasantly arranged in a recess of Boroughgate and known as St Anne's Hospital.

The hospital of St. Anne

Boroughgate, Appleby

The elegant dignity of Appleby's main street, Boroughgate, makes it the finest in the county, and happily, and appropriately, it is quiet and distant from the busy A.66. At the top of this lovely avenue is High Cross, a seventeenth-century column bearing the inscription RETAIN YOUR LOYALTY, PRESERVE YOUR RIGHTS.

The 12th-century castle keep, known as Caesar's Tower
Below *Low Cross and the Parish Church of Appleby*

The River Eden at Appleby

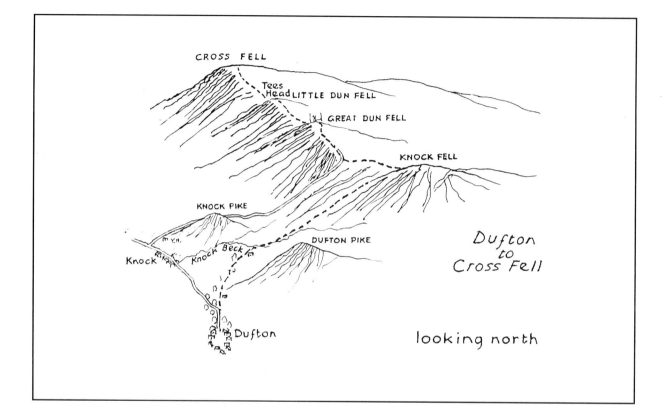

DUFTON is the springboard for the crossing of the highest of the Pennines, four summits over 2600 ft being visited on the next section of the Way, including the highest of all, Cross Fell. An early start is therefore essential and a fine day eminently preferable.

The village is left by the road to Knock, soon turning along a pleasant farm lane with the shapely cone of Dufton Pike ahead. All is quiet, rural and peaceful, but the scene would have been changed radically had a mad idea some years ago for the creation of a de-luxe sports centre around Dufton Pike with restaurants and hotels gone ahead. Fortunately it didn't, and contented cows still graze the fields. Which is as it should be.

Beyond the farm of Halsteads, a clapper bridge ensures a dry crossing of Great Rundale Beck and the ascent of Knock Fell starts in earnest. Higher, after fording Swindale Beck, a notice board too large to be missed and too officious to be ignored proclaims that the Moor House Nature Reserve is entered at this point, and states the conditions, positively negative, on which walkers will be tolerated: NO access without a permit except on a right of way; NO vehicles and NO dogs without written permission; DO NOT touch apparatus, traps, posts, etc.; DO NOT light fires or stoves; DO NOT drop lighted matches or cigarettes (cigars, pipes and 'pot' apparently OK?); KEEP AWAY from pools (ironic laughter). And not one 'please'. Presumably sneezing is allowed if really necessary.

Clapper bridge over Great Rundale Beck

Higher up the slope, following a line of cairns that seem to indicate the invisible right of way, a shallow ravine comes down on the left. This is artificial: it is a good example of a device known as a hush, formerly used in lead mining, whereby a small stream coming off the moors is dammed until a large volume of water is impounded; whereupon the dam is broken and the water is released to scour the slope below and, it is hoped, sweep away the vegetation and reveal any underlying veins of ore.

Dufton Pike

The summit of Knock Fell

Knock Old Man

On the later stages of the ascent, some vigorous springs and natural shakeholes looking like bomb craters add a little interest to the dull climb. The gradient eases as the large, well-built cairn of Knock Old Man is reached, and a simple stroll across a wide plateau decorated with many cairns leads to the highest point of Knock Fell which, at 2604 ft, is also the highest point of the Pennine Way thus far.

View from the summit of Knock Fell

Radar and weather station, Great Dun Fell

From the top of Knock Fell, it is a simple walk, slightly downhill, to the depression below the next summit, Great Dun Fell, which is readily identified by the radar masts sprouting from it and which are a perfect guide to direction; in mist, the aim is a little west of north. On this pathless mile, there are many evidences of old mines, some shakeholes in a band of limestone, and minor hollows that appear to be old workings.

In the depression, the tarmac road serving the radar station is joined, and it will occur to those of a crafty turn of mind that Knock Fell could have been omitted from the itinerary entirely, and an hour saved, simply by walking up this road from Knock village and, although not quite playing the game, this alternative is excusable in bad weather conditions. The road, the highest surfaced road in the country, is public. It is much used by skiers in snowy winters, lifting them in their cars to a height of 2500 ft without effort. Only the final few hundred yards are for the exclusive use of the station. On the way to the top, another spectacular example of prospecting for minerals by hushing is seen in Dunfell Hush, descending the slope on the right.

The radar station is always manned and I have found the staff invariably friendly, but as one who prefers his mountain tops to be quiet and unspoiled, it saddens me to see the top of Great Dun Fell, a proud 2780 ft, so defaced and debased by the paraphernalia of progress.

Considering the altitude and wild situation of these loftiest of the Pennines, the walk along the top to the next summit, Little Dun Fell, 2761 ft, is very easy on firm, dry turf. Little Dun Fell is sculptured on more slender lines than its neighbours, the ridge here being narrower and permitting aerial views down to the Eden Valley in the west and the sombre moors stretching eastwards towards Teesdale. There can be no doubt that this is the main watershed of northern England.

Without change of direction, the route traverses Little Dun Fell and descends to the marshy depression of Tees Head, where acquaintance is resumed with an old friend, the River Tees, here seen in infancy as a silver thread winding through surroundings of hopeless desolation. Across the depression, there is a sharp rise to the fringe of boulders that rings the plateau of Cross Fell like a necklace, and beyond a stroll to its summit which, at 2930 ft, is the highest point reached on the Pennine Way.

The summit of Little Dun Fell, looking to Cross Fell

The summit of Cross Fell

The top of Cross Fell, as befits the highest of the Pennines, has had this distinction recognised by its visitors, who have provided a display of assorted summit 'furniture' in the form of cairns and 'stone men' with a wind shelter and the inevitable Ordnance column crowning a broad grassy plateau.

The name of the fell, according to legend, derives from the erection of a cross on the summit by St Augustine to drive away the devils lurking there. The ruse seems to have proved successful, no evil spirits being in evidence today although their presence might be suspected on the occasions when a mighty wind, known locally as the Helm Wind, sweeps down the western slopes and leaves a trail of damage in the lowlands along the base of the fell.

The panorama on a day of clear visibility is magnificent, extending over all the northern counties of England and across the Solway Firth to the hills of Galloway. Superbly arrayed across the Eden Valley are the peaks of Lakeland, here seen for the last time on the journey but still inviting, still a tantalising magnet, yet now seeming a little reproachful: they are not accustomed to being bypassed.

Cross Fell is often sullen and capped by cloud but on a still day is quite benign, encouraging Wayfarers to linger and savour their achievement in reaching the apex of their journey in a mood of relaxed contemplation of their success. There is still much walking to be done, however, before they come face to face with a meal and a bed, and no time to lose.

Standing on the northern edge of the plateau, it would seem that the logical continuation of the route would follow the watershed northwards, persisting along the highest ground, crossing the Penrith–Alston road at its summit and thereafter keeping to the height of land until reaching the end of the Pennine range at the Carlisle–Newcastle gap. Instead, it turns soft, preferring to descend to the valley of the South Tyne and follow that river northwards for fifteen miles, shunning the high ground completely in favour of an uncharacteristic ramble along a valley.

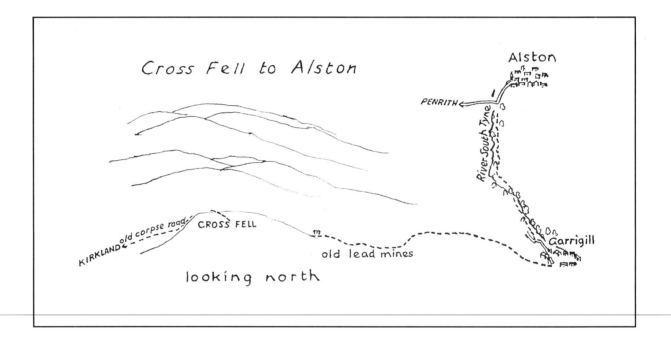

FROM Cross Fell, the next stage of the journey is to the east, but beelines in that direction pass through an area of open mine shafts, snares that could end once and for all ambitions of completing the Pennine Way. The official route is more roundabout, descending north from the plateau through the necklace of stones to a clear track running below. This is an old corpse road, formerly used to convey the dead of Garrigill for interment in consecrated ground at Kirkland in the Eden Valley: an arduous journey of ten miles at high altitudes. There must have been a very good reason why the corpses were not taken to last resting places at nearby Alston. In thick weather, walkers have cause to be grateful to the dead of Garrigill for the funeral processions have left a distinct and foolproof path all the way to Garrigill.

This path is followed to the right, descending past a ruined cottage that has been repaired to provide a shelter for stormbound travellers, and then enters a devastated area, the site of an abandoned lead mine.

If half an hour can be spared, it may profitably be spent in an exploration of the workings of the lead mine which, although derelict, has much of surface interest remaining and gives an insight into the methods of operation. Caution is necessary and no holes should be entered.

Relics of the old Mines on Cross Fell

A dry level (a main access to the mine, in some cases serviced by light railways for the extraction of ore and spoil)

Wet levels (conduits for draining water from the mine to the open hillside as an alternative to pumping, to prevent floods)

An air shaft

A horse-drawn truck or sled

Lead mining is amongst the oldest of the Pennine industries. From chance finds in some of the mines and from excavations in their camps, it is known that the Romans worked in these hills for lead, and there is some evidence that they exploited surface workings used by the native Britons earlier. Their operations were not on a large scale, there being little domestic use for the mineral, but the industry subsequently increased considerably with the demand for lead as a roofing material in the building of churches, castles, abbeys and monasteries throughout the country in the succeeding centuries. In later times, technical improvements assisted in the extraction and smelting processes, resulting in greater output to meet the growing demand for industrial purposes. The peak of activity was reached in the nineteenth century, many thousands of men being employed at the main centres around Alston and Swaledale, but towards its end cheaper supplies from foreign sources caused so severe a check to home production that most of the mines became uneconomical to operate and were closed. Today, almost all are derelict and abandoned, rotting monuments to an industry that perished, a few surviving for the extraction of fluorspar and barytes, once considered as waste spoil but now regarded as valuable agents in steel making and other manufactures.

All who walk the Pennine Way will forever afterwards have imperishable memories of their accomplishment, but a more tangible reminder is offered by the liberal scatterings of beautiful blue crystals of fluorspar along the track after leaving the mine: a small collection of these will make a lovely miniature cairn for the mantelpiece at home, wife permitting, and be a permanent symbol of remembrance.

Also of interest alongside the track is a landmark the horses pulling the carts loved to see: an iron watering trough.

These features apart, there is nothing worthy of note until a view of the valley of the South Tyne gradually opens ahead. Even tired legs will enjoy the four exhilarating miles from the mine to Garrigill, the track being unmistakable and becoming enclosed by walls in the later stages. It is good to see habitations and trees again, the first since leaving Dufton, as the track finally descends sharply to Garrigill.

The few buildings of Garrigill are pleasantly arranged around an open green with the River South Tyne meandering amongst trees nearby and lofty fells around, an oasis of greenery and a welcome sight after a day spent on the bleak moors. There is an inn with a good reputation and possibly cottage accommodation, but walkers blessed with reserves of energy prefer to undertake the four miles of riverside walking to the town of Alston.

The valley of the South Tyne at Garrigill

Garrigill

A path leaves the road at Garrigill and immediately comes alongside the River South Tyne, which at this point has already travelled five miles from its source at Tyne Head, where it is within a mile of the Tees, and is of considerable width. This river is destined to join the River North Tyne, met later on the journey, their mingled waters then flowing as the River Tyne into the North Sea at Newcastle. There is now a definite feeling that the wild moors of the Pennines have been left behind, that a very different territory lies ahead, friendly and inhabited, and that the ultimate north of England has been entered.

The path keeps closely to the left bank of the river for two miles and then crosses over it by a footbridge near Sillyhall Farm.

From Sillyhall, the path persists along the right bank of the river through a succession of small fields and never far from the company of the rushing water, which hereabouts has widened its bed quite considerably to accommodate the floods that occasionally surge down from the hills.

The path then develops into a pleasant wooded lane, a favourite walk of Alstonians and their dogs, and reaches the Penrith road, A.686, down a flight of steps at Alston Bridge.

The River South Tyne at Sillyhall

Below *Looking back from Sillyhall*

Alston Bridge

The Pennine Way crosses Alston Bridge and continues alongside the river, but few long-distance walkers miss the opportunity of a visit to the small town half a mile up the road to the right to replenish the rucksack or enjoy a carouse at one of the inns or secure a night's lodgings, these facilities not again being in full supply until Bellingham is reached forty-two miles further on.

Alston claims to be the highest market town in England, its altitude exceeding 1000 ft; its situation is isolated from other communities over a very extensive area, its links being a network of roads, some with bus services, and formerly it had a railway station at the terminus of a tenuous branch line, which has not survived. A Youth Hostel is a recent innovation.

Last century, Alston was the centre of a large lead mining area, this industry bringing prosperity to the town and being responsible for its development to present proportions. The nearby hills are scarred and pock-marked with abandoned workings, but the town itself has recovered from adversity and is a busy centre of shopping and commerce.

Alston is a good example of a town that came into being without the help or interference of town planners and has since fended them off. It is a delightfully haphazard huddle of buildings, many of distinction, and narrow alleys, arranged along a steep main street, a notable feature being the pillared market cross.

Alston is insular, yet friendly: a remembered place.

Market Place, Alston

For the next ten miles, the Pennine Way proceeds down the narrow valley of the River South Tyne on a route closely interwoven with a road, the river, the Maiden Way of the Romans, a derelict railway track and lines of poles, all tightly confined between encroaching heights and jostling for space, often changing their positions relative to the others. This section is rather bitty and messy but its intricacies can always be resolved by reference to the various lines of communications all heading the same way, so that there is little danger of straying seriously. Nevertheless, now that the railway has gone, these ten miles would give easy and trouble-free walking if they were to be re-charted along the railway track.

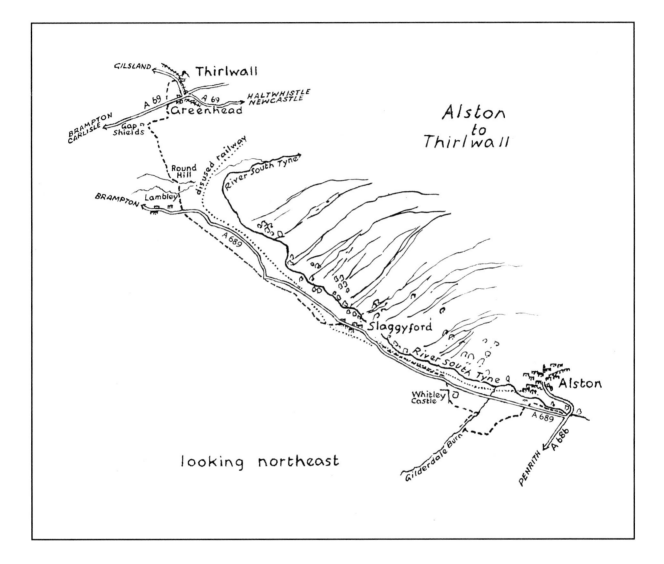

THE surroundings are pleasant and the river attractive, but nowhere is there the charm and excitement of Teesdale.

Furthermore, there is awareness that throughout, high above on the left, is the lofty skyline of the final range of the Pennines, cruelly forsaken for a soft option and looking down in disapproval at the truants wending their way through farmyards and fields and cows. Up there, they would have had good honest peat on their boots, not manure, and they would have been able to stride out in open spaces and not had to fiddle with stiles and gates, and they would have heard the cry of the curlew. Up there are the last hills of the Pennines, and they are being ignored. Shame!

Alston from the river

Below *Gilderdale Burn*

The Way is resumed from the bridge at Alston by a pleasant path along the left bank of the river, where there is a good view of the town on its hill. Then the A.689 is crossed and, surprisingly and unnecessarily, the route goes uphill, making a long detour around three sides of an imaginary square before returning to the road further along. The merit of this deviation is not clear, nor is the path. Gilderdale Burn, draining a vast moorland expanse, is crossed by a footbridge and followed down to a cart track that skirts the earthworks of Whitley Castle, a Roman fort notable for its series of earthen ramparts, and then returns to the road.

It is encouraging to note that streams, which in Derbyshire are called 'brooks' and in Yorkshire 'becks' are now within an area of Scottish influence and known as 'burns'. Can't be far to the Border!

Whitley Castle

Whitley Castle was built by the Romans as a garrisoned fort to defend the Maiden Way, a road they laid across the Pennines from their fort at Kirkby Thore to Carvoran near Hadrian's Wall. The earthworks cover an area of nearly nine acres and are notable for the earthen ramparts and ditches surrounding a large flat platform elevated above and commanding a splendid view of the valley. This is the best-preserved fort of its type in the country. The line of the Maiden Way is not clear hereabouts, having been overlaid, but its general course is obvious and becomes clear on the ground further down the valley where it is adopted by the Pennine Way over a distance of three miles.

After leaving Whitley Castle, the A.689 is reached and crossed at once to enter a succession of small fields, provided with stiles, passing occasional farms. The path is now on the line of the Maiden Way, although not recognisable as such, and runs alongside the old railway track. This section is tedious, a habitat of cows, but improves when the path leads beneath a viaduct to the river bank. Here are the first open views of the South Tyne since Alston and it is now seen to have matured, having carved a wide bed and pebbly beaches along a tree-fringed and wooded course. Here it is beautiful.

The River South Tyne near Slaggyford

Slaggyford

Below *Burnstones*

The company of the river is not enjoyed for long, the route rejoining the road and going with it into Slaggyford, the only village in the valley and a possible provider of refreshments.

At Slaggyford, the Way leaves the road by a lane passing the village chapel and crossing beneath a railway viaduct. From here onwards, the path remains consistently to the west of road, railway and river for some miles, but is again complicated by small enclosures and simplified by stiles until the little complex of buildings at Burnstones is reached, one of them a former inn and the whole forming a nice grouping amongst splendid trees.

Burnstones marks the end of the fragrant farmyards, the well-manured dairy pastures and the many individual cowclaps. Now shoulders can be squared again and the gaze fixed ahead instead of watching where the feet are treading. From this point onwards for the next three miles, the path adopts the Maiden Way exactly and is a joy to walk, heading due north as straight as an arrow and without hindrances to progress.

Gradually the route emerges from the confines of the valley, the slopes on either side losing height to reveal a widening view ahead that extends far into the distance. This is another threshold, another landscape, the beginning of another chapter in the saga of the Pennine Way. Now can be seen over the declining foothills of the Pennines, the shadowy outline of Scottish hills beyond the desert of Spadeadam Waste, a danger zone where weapons of war are tested. Nearer, a continuous depression in the landscape marks the Carlisle–Newcastle gap, a busy trade artery threaded by the River Irthing and, extending eastwards from it, the low ridges that carry the Roman Wall.

The A.689 is crossed for the last time as it escapes from the valley and turns sharp west to Brampton. The River South Tyne and the disused railway trend away to the east. These close companions over the past ten miles pass from sight. In open country again, the route continues north.

The Maiden Way

Hartley Burn

Although the distant prospect is exciting, the immediate foreground is less inviting, the devastated area of the abandoned Lambley Colliery having first to be crossed through a shambles of derelict buildings, air shafts, kilns and clay pits for which the County Council has put forward a scheme for redevelopment not to the liking of nearby residents. Beyond is a series of low rounded hills with streams flowing between eastwards to join the River South Tyne, the two principal waterways being Hartley Burn and Kellah Burn, the former attractively wooded and both having footbridges.

This section is complicated, but maintains a constant direction slightly west of north, passing isolated farmsteads and crossing areas of undulating moorland. Looking back will be seen the abrupt butt end of the high Pennines, the end of the range, and it will be appreciated that the route is now passing through lesser foothills that decline finally to the depression ahead. When the farm of Gap Shields is reached a sharp turn east leads to a cart track that goes down to the A.69, the highway between Carlisle and Newcastle.

The A.69 is crossed into fields that bear traces of the ancillary works forming part of the defensive fortifications of the Roman Wall. This is a great moment for imaginative minds. Here at last, the route reaches the territory where the Romans built their greatest monument along a strip of land extending from the Solway Firth to the North Sea, a mighty wall to repel Scots invaders, and for those with antiquarian and historical interests, this remarkable undertaking must rank as the greatest highlight of all.

The first evidence to be met in these fields is a lateral hollow along which ran the military road, or Stanegate, used to service the forts on the Wall, and just beyond is the shallow ditch known as the Vallum. There is no sign as yet of the Wall itself, which hereabouts was later plundered for its conveniently ready cut stones.

The path travels east in company with the Vallum to reach the road B.6318 linking Gilsland and Greenhead and carrying the Carlisle–Newcastle bus service and the railway along a valley dominated by Thirlwall Castle.

The last of the high Pennines

Roman remains at Gilsland

On arrival at the B.6318, after walking nearly twenty miles since leaving Alston (and two hundred since leaving Edale) overnight accommodation will probably be required, and there are possibilities of this at the cottages below Thirlwall Castle, or at Greenhead along the road to the right, or, although off route, at the pleasant village of Gilsland along the road to the left. Gilsland has attractions other than those concerned with beds and breakfasts, for in the village can be seen well-preserved portions of the Roman Wall, some fragments appearing in the gardens of modern villas and being valued as unique ornaments nearly two thousand years old. Gilsland's river is the Irthing, which flows west to join the River Eden and ultimately the Solway Firth. All other streams met since leaving Cross Fell have flowed east, including the one at Thirlwall, a long mile away, so that the main watershed occurs between the two places although this is not obvious on the ground. Gilsland is in Cumbria, Thirlwall in the Northumberland National Park.

The River Irthing at Gilsland

The Irthing effectively terminates the Pennines. They go no further north. If the Pennine Way was true to its name, it should end here, with a final flourish along the Roman Wall to give the walk a well-defined and worthy final objective. As approved by the Countryside Commission, it is a part-Pennine and part-Cheviot Way. My opinion is that the walk should start at the southern extremity of the Pennines, say at the Staffordshire Roaches, and reach Edale by way of Axe Edge and Rushup Edge, giving a grand high-level start, and end at the Roman Wall. Then it would truly be a Pennine Way, covering the whole length of the Pennines and nothing but the Pennines. It seems to me a mistake to continue the walk beyond the Roman Wall into a land of anti-climax in the form of interminable conifer forests, many having been established or extended since the route was first devised. At the end, the Cheviot Hills are traversed for half their length; these provide good walking but deserve a Cheviot Way all their own.

However, it is not for the troops to reason why; theirs is but to do or die along the route decreed by the generals. The Way is resumed at Thirlwall without further argument.

Now for the Roman Wall, the greatest and most impressive of the monuments created by the Romans during their occupation of the country. It provides a fascinating study for archaeologists and historians, continuing excavations revealing new discoveries, and even to those visitors with no specialist knowledge, an examination of the plentiful remains and especially a traverse along the Wall is an emotive experience long to be remembered.

The Wall was commissioned by the Emperor Hadrian in AD 122 as a barrier to keep at bay marauding tribes from the north who could not be subdued by invasion and conquest, and is often referred to as Hadrian's Wall. Seventy-three miles in length, it extended from the Solway Firth to the North Sea, taking advantage of natural obstacles and in the middle section running along the rim of an escarpment of basaltic rock, the Whin Sill, where north-facing cliffs formed an effective defence and commanded far-reaching views over the area from which attacks were to be expected. The Wall, originally over ten feet in height and six feet thick, was built of square-cut stones, and provided at intervals with forts and mile-castles and sentry turrets, many still to be seen on a traverse of the fortifications.

Close to the north side of the Wall, a ditch was cut as an added defence except in places where steep cliffs made it unnecessary.

On the south side of the Wall, a military way connected the forts to facilitate movements of the garrisons and supplies, and the line of this can still be traced, and at varying distances from the Wall was another ditch, the Vallum. This one is continuous and plain to see, its purpose probably to mark the military boundary and to keep away civilian intruders. Also on the south side was a Roman road, the Stanegate. The modern B.6318 that runs parallel to the Wall in a remarkably straight line, was originally an eighteenth-century turnpike, and is commonly called the Military Road.

The ten miles between Thirlwall and Housesteads along the course of the Wall is a wonderful journey, full of incident. In places, the Wall has disappeared, having been robbed of its stones by subsequent builders, or quarried out of existence, but long sections have survived although reduced in height, and can be walked alongside, or on the broad top, with ease. These ten stimulating miles form the next stage of the Pennine Way.

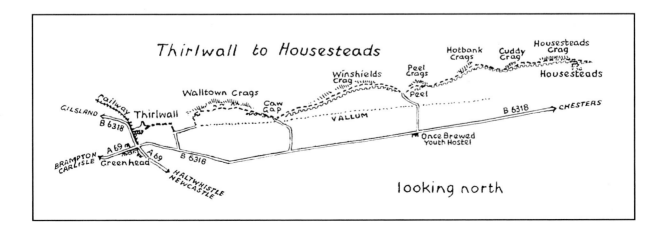

FROM the B.6318 at Thirlwall, the railway and the tree-fringed Tipalt Burn are crossed in a charming dell and, beyond some cottages, a steep climb leads up alongside the conspicuous ruins of Thirlwall Castle. This is a fourteenth-century pele tower, built in part of stones from the Roman Wall which originally passed through the dell but of which there is nothing remaining. A rare aberration of the Ordnance Survey, who name the castle 'Thirwall', occurs on their maps here.

The Pennine Way turns east from Thirlwall Castle on a ridge, and here meets the Roman ditch for the first time, the path proceeding along its north bank; the south bank is occupied by an English wall superimposed on the foundations of the vanished Roman Wall. Nearby, down the hillside on the right, is the site of the fort of Carvoran at the junction of the Stanegate and the Maiden Way but almost all evidences have disappeared. Ahead, the route is interrupted by a large quarry that has carved a great hollow out of the ridge, destroying the Roman Wall in the process, and beyond is the serrated escarpment of Walltown Crags, a series of ups and downs known as the Nine Nicks of Thirlwall.

Opposite *Thirlwall Castle*   *Walltown Crags*

First sight of the Wall

The quarry is skirted at its lower end and, when clear of it, the slope beyond is climbed to the escarpment of Walltown Crags, and there, in a dip, is the Wall at last—a thrilling moment.

This particular section has recently been repaired to arrest further decay and, although sadly reduced from its original height, is a typical remnant with plinth projections. Constructional details, however, differ in other sections of the Wall.

Whenever I hear mention of the Roman Wall, or see references to it, the circumstances of my first visit are brought vividly to mind. It was in the autumn of 1938 when the constant talk of an imminent war and fire drills and air raid precautions and other preparations for conflict, made me and everybody else very apprehensive and unsettled, and we were not helped by the fanatical ravings of Hitler on the radio. I had ten days' holiday due to me and decided to get away from the disturbing atmosphere by walking along the Pennines from Lancashire to the Roman Wall, which I had never seen, and back by a different route. This I did, staying overnight at cottages, but the feeling of unease persisted.

I remember particularly one night at Muker, when I was harboured by an old lady who lived alone. After supper in the flicker of an oil lamp, she switched on her little wireless set, and there again was Hitler, screaming threats louder than ever, his patience obviously exhausted. It was a frightening experience, not the sort of thing one expects in lovely Swaledale. I stood at the front door, looking across the valley; it was a still night with a canopy of stars and a profound silence over all. Hitler seemed strangely unreal . . . At Hexham a few days later, I looked out of the bedroom window on a sunny morning and saw outside a newspaper shop a placard with the one word PEACE. Mr Chamberlain had been to Munich and quietened the man, to everybody's great relief. But it was a strange holiday. In the ten days, I did not meet another walker. I went to the Roman Wall and marvelled at it. It was a relic of another invasion, but that was nearly two thousand years before. It held no terrors. I thought it was wonderful, and still do.

Writing this reminiscence has reminded me that upon returning home I wrote a book about the incidents of this holiday under the title of *A Pennine Journey*. Only half a dozen friends ever read the manuscript, which they thought a classic, or so they said. It has lain in a drawer for the past forty-five years. Someday I will dig it out of its dust and have it published.

But I digress.

Following the notched crest of Walltown Crags is not a rewarding exercise as far as the hunt for things Roman is concerned. The remains of the Wall are fragmentary along the escarpment, and the Way prefers to bypass the extreme edge by adopting the line of the military road until the cliffs are passed. Then the path returns to the ridge and it will be noted that the ditch is again in evidence when the escarpment terminates and the natural defence provided by crags is lost. The walking is now on the actual foundations of the Wall, which occurs above ground only at intervals, but a good example of a surviving wall-turret is soon reached.

Turret 44B

Milecastles were built adjoining the south side of the Wall at intervals of a Roman mile (1620 yards) and between them two turrets were erected also abutting the Wall and spaced at equal distances, these being used as look-out towers. For identification purposes, the milecastles and turrets have been numbered by modern historians from east to west. The turret here reached is No 44B and appears after No 44A and Milecastle 44 when approached from the east. Many of the turrets have fallen into complete decay. Although its walls are diminished to five feet in height, Turret 44B is one of the best examples remaining, its plan of construction being clear. Some good specimens of milecastles will be met later in the walk.

The Whin Sill, east from Walltown Crags

Continuing along the undulating ridge, the Way passes by the side of an English wall built largely with Roman stones and, after more switchbacks, goes past the fort of Aesica, where excavations have been undertaken, and the farm of Great Chesters; then, with the ditch again alongside and the Wall in evidence in a reduced state, the Way descends to Burnhead Farm and a gap in the ridge crossed by a minor road. Beyond is a quarry that has destroyed the next section of the Wall, and the escarpment of Cawfield Crags.

Cawfield Crags

Looking west along the Wall at Winshields Crag

Below *The summit of Winshields Crag*

Along the rim of Cawfield Crags, the Wall resumes and is in good condition following restoration, and here is Milecastle 42, the best preserved of the milecastles thus far seen. A descent is made to Caw Gap, also crossed by a minor road, and after a further depression the ascent is made to the highest point of the Wall on Winshields Crag at 1230 ft, the Wall now being a constant companion, and heather making attractive surroundings. The traverse of Winshields Crag is very pleasant, apart from its historical associations and fine views, and indeed is akin to fell walking at its best.

View from the summit of Winshields Crag

The top of Winshields Crag excels as a viewpoint. The all-round panorama is magnificent. Across the Solway Firth can be seen the hills of southern Scotland, and far to the south Cross Fell can be seen, with a final glimpse of the fells of the Lake District. This is a view of great detail that can be studied for hours on a clear day. What always impresses me here is not only the wide landscapes with their distant horizons but the wonderful skyscapes, especially on a day of cumulus clouds, that seem to encompass this airy perch. Winshields Crag is a good place to be when the air is still and the views extensive.

Nobody is likely to dispute my opinion that the Wall is at its finest in the four miles from Winshields Crag to Housesteads, where it is almost continuous, passes through glorious scenery and provides excellent walking on its broad top or alongside. Because other people obviously agree with me, and because this section is easily accessible its one demerit is that it is often over-populated by walkers.

A place of popular resort, encouraged by a car park, is at Peel, where the path from Winshields Crag comes down to a road crossing. Here the Wall is substantial and steps have been provided so that even the infirm can mount to its wide top, a debatable amenity.

From this point onwards to Housesteads, only a minimum of written description of the route is necessary, the Wall itself being a perfect guide, and photographs give a much better indication of the route and its environs than words.

It should be mentioned, however, that the road at Peel, followed south, gives quick access to Once Brewed, a Youth Hostel formerly a farm, and Twice Brewed, still an inn, and there is only a remote chance of finding any other night's lodgings until Bellingham is reached eighteen miles further.

Looking east along the Whin Sill from Winshields Crag

Peel Crags

A steep scramble leads to the top of Peel Crags; here the Wall is in good shape. Beyond, Milecastle 39 is reached. This is one of the best preserved; note the gateways.

From Milecastle 39, the lake of Crag Lough is in sight ahead with the vertical cliffs of Highshield Crag towering over its waters. When above these crags, which form one of the most popular of Northumbrian climbing grounds, there are sensational aerial views of the lake glimpsed down breaches in the cliffs. This is the most graphic situation on the course of the Wall. No need for a ditch here!

Milecastle 39　　　　　　　　　　　　　　　Opposite *Highshield Crag and Crag Lough*

Crag Lough from Highshield Crag

Beyond Highshield Crag, the Wall climbs over Hotbank Crags and then descends into Rapishaw Gap, where the Pennine Way departs from it and heads north. But by continuing along the Wall for a short mile further, the impressive remains of the fort of Housesteads will be reached, and this is a highlight too interesting to miss. The detour and return to Rapishaw Gap will take an hour, and regard must be had to the time of day, Bellingham still being a long march of fourteen miles distant.

The direct climb out of Rapishaw Gap is made rather difficult by a line of low crags that interrupt the Wall but can be easily circumvented to arrive on Cuddy's Crags, where the Wall is rejoined and which has an excellent view forward to the wooded height of Housesteads Crags much favoured by photographers, with the Wall seen aiming unerringly ahead and wide enough to be walked on the whole way.

Rapishaw Gap and Cuddy's Crags

Milecastle 37, passed before reaching the trees above Housesteads Crags, is one of the best examples surviving. The Wall enters the trees, its top making an excellent path, and emerges at Housesteads Fort, the Roman Borcovicium. This is the best preserved and one of the two most visited forts adjoining the Wall and is a wonderful stimulus to the imagination.

The usual approach is from a large car park off the Military Road, B.6318, a favourite halt of sight-seeing coach parties, a short climb on a beaten track leading up to a museum and entrance through the south gateway. An admission charge is made to those who arrive by the orthodox path from the car park, a toll that can be avoided by unscrupulous walkers who come by way of the Wall and enter the precincts through the north gateway. Members of the National Trust get in free.

Opposite *Housesteads Crags from Cuddy's Crags*   Above *The Wall to Housesteads*

The fort covers an area of five acres, and although of course ruinous, the arrangement of the various quarters is clearly defined. A tour of the site, which is rectangular in plan, discloses the four gateways, one on each side, the headquarters building, the commandant's house, the barracks of the garrison, the latrines and, best of all, the granaries.

Housesteads is an education.

Housesteads: the south gate

As I've mentioned earlier, I think that the Pennine Way should end here at Housesteads, on a high note. The Roman Wall is an obvious climax to a walk along the Pennines, being situated at the end of the range, and Housesteads would provide a grand finale, the supreme moment of achievement and an objective far worthier of attainment than the village green at Kirk Yetholm.

But it doesn't. Climax is followed by an anti-climax sixty miles long, no part of it related in any way to the Pennines. From here on, the Pennine Way is a misnomer.

The granaries

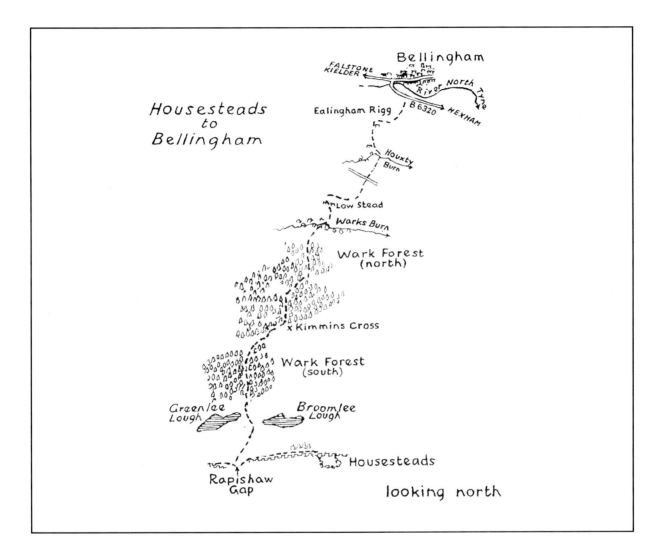

THERE is an affliction known as Wall Fever that affects many visitors to the old fortifications of the Roman Wall, and results from enthusiasm, imagination and a passionate urge to discover more of its secrets. This is a healthy and a rewarding pursuit.

But the Pennine Way must come first. 'On to Bellingham' must be the cry. Yet it is hard to leave the Wall. Few will continue the journey north without looking back.

Steps must be retraced to Rapishaw Gap, where an old droveway goes down north into a depression containing two natural lakes, Greenlee Lough and Broomlee Lough, commonly referred to, with Crag Lough, as the Lakes of Northumberland. These are pleasant sheets of water, a habitat of waterfowl. Greenlee Lough has the site of a Roman camp on its south shore.

The Northumberland Lakes: Above *Greenlee Lough*   Below *Broomlee Lough*

Beyond the two loughs and a ruined farm, the path rises to enter the gloomy confines of Wark Forest, which is in three sections with intervals of open ground between and extends for interminable miles forward. Walking on the forest roads is fast and easy, dry underfoot and deadly dull, with many bifurcations that are confusing and could lead walkers astray unless the line of the route is watched carefully. There are no landmarks. Every yard of the way in these forests is like the next with nothing to see but crippled conifers.

Looking back to the Whin Sill ridge

Nobody loves trees more than I do, but for these wretched spruces there can only be compassion. Down in the forest nothing stirs. There is no bird song. There is silence and the atmosphere of a graveyard. One feels sorry for these densely-packed trees, not one growing as it would wish and living the miserable existence of battery hens. Every tree starts life wanting to be a noble and beautiful specimen, but these poor things are deliberately starved of sunlight even from birth. Except around the fringes of the forest they are skeletons, without foliage, their branches withered, barely surviving in the darkness of a tomb, the intention of the planters being that they should grow tall as they fight for air and light, and so develop a commercial value. They grow, not as trees but as poles. This is man's design, not nature's. It is always man that commits the affronts to a natural and fulfilled existence, of animals as well as trees. He is top dog in this world, and don't you forget it.

The forests are the dominating feature of the landscape between the Roman Wall and the Cheviot Hills.

The Border Forest Park, established in 1955, is the largest of Britain's planted forests, and yet probably the least known because of its remoteness from centres of population and tourist routes. It occupies a vast tract of reclaimed heath on both sides of the Scottish border, extending with other adjacent forests outside the Park boundary over an area of nearly 300 square miles, formerly largely an uncultivated wilderness with a few isolated habitations and a sparse and declining population.

Very different is the picture today. For mile after mile, these rolling moors have sprouted a mantle of growing timber, mainly the hardy Sitka spruce, with open areas left for husbandry and sheep farming. Within the forests, new villages have been created for the men who construct the roads, plant and maintain the crop, and ultimately reap the harvest—after a wait of some forty years. The coming of the forests has brought life and prosperity to a district that was dying of poverty, and hope where there was no hope.

The transformation is complete.

The Park is formed by six principal forests: Kielder, Wark, Redesdale, Kershope, Wauchope, Newcastleton.   The Pennine Way skirts the eastern fringe of the group, entering and passing through the Wark and Redesdale forests for a few miles on gravel roads or rides (fire breaks).

Walking in coniferous forests is not everybody's cup of tea. Although fast progress is possible on the forest roads, some people experience a feeling of oppressiveness amounting almost to claustrophobia, and others not so affected quickly tire of the sameness of the surroundings, the lack of interest or variety in the regimented avenues of spruce, the loss of a sense of direction and the absence of breezes flowing free. It is always a relief after being shut in to get out.

A forest road, Wark Forest

The Border Forests

Willowbog Farm

Forest walking is the antithesis of fell walking, for in the one there is a severe confinement, a rigid line of march, a lack of living creatures, an absence of bird song, inability to see far ahead or look around; but in the other there is freedom, freedom to wander and explore, to look into far distances, to select a line of march and vary it at will, and there is the friendly companionship of animals and birds in the open spaces. The forest is a prison, the fell is liberty. The one is artificial, as man made it; the other unspoilt, as nature made it.

Emergence from Wark Forest (south) is like coming out of a tunnel into sunlight. Landscapes and horizons can be seen again. At the point of exit, there is a clear view ahead across the open moor of Hawk Side to the central part of the forest a mile distant and this is reached near the remains of Kimmins Cross where, according to legend, a northern chieftain named Cummings was slain by sons of King Arthur.

The central section is shorter, ending after a mile at a minor road in a clearing around Ladyhill Farm, from which the north part of Wark Forest is entered.

The north forest is traversed on grassy rides to open and undulating country with a rural flavour. A small stream is forded and from a hillock beyond, a descent is made to the pleasant valley of Warks Burn, quite the prettiest spot met since leaving the Roman Wall. The stream, already the size of a young river, is a principal tributary of the River North Tyne, and is crossed by a footbridge in a charming dell. 'Wark' is a common place name hereabouts, occurring in Wark village, Wark Bridge, Wark Common and Wark Forest, but curiously the name of the stream has an 's' added, making it Warks Burn. However, notwithstanding this inconsistency, the waterside scenery is a refreshing change and it is good to see deciduous trees growing naturally and obviously enjoying their environment.

The Valley of Warks Burn   Opposite *Warks Burn*

Horneystead

Below *Low Stead*

An open and pastoral countryside with farmsteads follows from Warks Burn and in this rural setting it is evident that there has been little change for centuries in the tranquillity of life. Most of the old farmhouses, mellowed with age, have a character and distinction that seems beyond the capacity of modern builders to attain. Even the ruin of Horneystead, met first after leaving the footbridge, is handsome despite decay: parts have recently been restored and re-occupied.

A minor road is reached, followed for a short distance and then left to cross fields to Low Stead, an attractive complex of farm buildings, and here one joins a lane that continues the Way north.

Houxty Burn   Overleaf *View from Shitlington Crags*

The lane leaving Low Stead is followed for a mile, and then, at a T-junction with a motor road, a field path leads down to Houxty Burn, meandering pleasantly along a little wooded valley. It is crossed by a footbridge to the farm of Shitlington Hall, where one wonders why its earthy name is preferred to the former Shotlyngton Hall. From it, a rising path leads up to a line of low cliffs rejoicing in the name of Shitlington Crags, where one wonders afresh. These rocks are easily scaled to reach the heathery heights of Ealingham Rigg.

Ealingham Rigg is a delightful promenade, its carpet of heather making a welcome change after the many miles of forests and fields. And at last Bellingham is in view, nestling snugly in the wide valley of the River North Tyne with a background of rolling moors. To the west stretch the vast Kielder forests. The prospect is wide, revealing in detail a landscape not before seen on the journey.

Ealingham Rigg merits a long halt to absorb the new landscapes ahead, but for those who arrive on this fine vantage point with tired limbs and ravenous appetites, the magnet that attracts their gaze will be Bellingham, and an early acquaintance with its shops and drinking parlours can be made by descending the hillside to the B.6320, the Hexham road, and following this to the left to enter the main street over a handsome river bridge.

The valley of the North Tyne from Ealingham Rigg

The River North Tyne at Bellingham

Bellingham, unexpectedly pronounced Bellinjam, is little more than a large village but earns the status of a town by reason of its market and a general acceptance as the 'capital' of the valley of the North Tyne. There are shops in variety here, hotels, bed and breakfast cottages, a Youth Hostel and an interesting twelfth-century church, with the wide river providing a delightful amenity. Once it had a branch railway of scenic charm running down the length of the valley from the Waverley line at Riccarton to Hexham. As the only community of any size within a very wide radius, Bellingham is an important centre of activity in a strategic situation at the entrance to the Kielder forest area, which is fast becoming a tourist attraction and well worth exploring if a day can be spared.

After the loneliness of the day's long march, Pennine Wayfarers will find it a little strange to be in the company of traffic and people going about their business or gossiping in groups, of ladies pushing prams and children playing, all indifferent to the triumphal entry into their midst of walkers who have come on foot all the way from the Roman Wall. It is a return to civilisation, and with a meal and a bed imminent, it will readily be conceded that civilisation has its merits.

I remember dragging myself into Bellingham on a scorching hot day after walking from the Twice Brewed Inn and going badly astray in the maze of Wark Forest; I was utterly weary and completely dehydrated, urging myself over the last few miles with a promise of ice cream in copious quantities. I arrived in the late afternoon just as the shops were closing but went into a café and ordered half a crown's worth of ice cream in a dish to eat on the premises. At first the shopkeeper demurred, saying he wanted to lock up and go home, but he took pity on my obvious distress, partly feigned, and served me with a slab of ice cream as big as a loaf. Half a crown's worth of ice cream in those days would cost three or four pounds today. With the shopkeeper meaningfully consulting his watch every few seconds, I wolfed the lot. . . . It was a silly thing to do. Such an ice-cold douche on an overheated stomach was bound to do me no good at all, but mercifully had a delayed action for two days until I was back at home. Then for a week I suffered for my folly.

The main street, Bellingham   Opposite *Hareshaw Linn*

The great scenic showplace of Bellingham is the lovely waterfall of Hareshaw Linn, reached by a charming walk through a long wooded glen on a good path with six footbridges, the whole adopted as a Nature Trail. The stream descending the glen is a tributary of the River North Tyne.

Originally, the Pennine Way took this line out of Bellingham but it was changed to the present less attractive route, which is roughly parallel. Unfortunately, there is no right of way linking one with the other and Hareshaw Linn is therefore an off-route detour, which requires a complete retracing of steps and adding four miles to the journey. Pennine Wayfarers who still retain a spark of romance and poetry in their souls and an appreciation of beauty after all they have suffered are recommended to make an extra effort to see the Linn; for others whose higher feelings have been shrivelled by their day after day agonies, it would be a waste of valuable time.

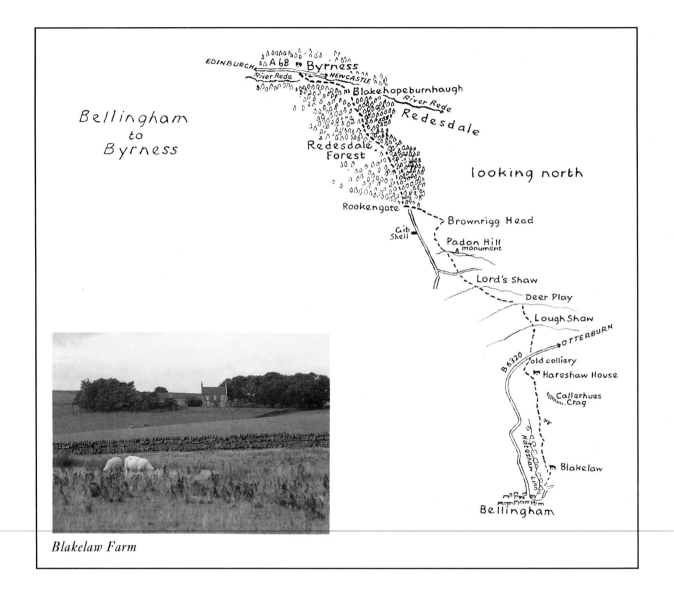

Blakelaw Farm

BEFORE leaving Bellingham, it is prudent to check the contents of the rucksack, since there is no further opportunity to obtain supplies before Journey's End, forty miles distant.

The first objective is Blakelaw Farm, reached by a rising access road, and from here a track contours the hillside ahead, grass giving way to bracken and heather, with occasional crags up on the right and the wooded defile of Hareshaw Linn down on the left, the aim being the grounds of Hareshaw House at the head of the valley. Beyond, the old wagonway of a disused colliery, which closed in the 1950s after operating for 200 years, leads across the site of demolished miners' cottages to the B.6320 road.

The B.6320 is crossed to an open moorland forming an indefinite and undulating ridge that maintains an altitude in excess of a thousand feet for the next five miles and rises in that distance to five named summits, none of them distinctive. This section is featureless and without a fence or a wall to act as a guide for most of the way and, in the absence of a distinct path, care and compass are needed in misty conditions. The first summit reached is Lough Shaw, 1102 ft, and the second Deer Play, 1183 ft, neither of them exciting and having no landmarks other than shooting butts. 'Shaw' means wood, 'Lough' means lake, 'Deer' means deer, but none of these things will be seen.

The summit of Deer Play

Above *The summit of Lough Shaw*

From Deer Play, the route turns north-west over marshy ground to the summit of Lord's Shaw, 1167 ft and then descends to cross a moorland road that offers an escape from the ridge in the event of bad weather: if the road is followed down to the left and then north, passing the lonely farm of Gib Shiel and entering Redesdale Forest, Byrness will be reached without difficulty; indeed this was the proposed route of the Pennine Way until 1961 when it was altered to avoid road walking. The revised version crosses the road and continues the ridge by ascending to the next summit, Padon Hill, 1240 ft, the highest point reached since leaving Cross Fell.

The summit of Padon Hill

Padon Hill has a conspicuous landmark in the form of an obelisk, visible from afar. It is sited east of the ridge fence, off-route, but it is worth making the short detour to see the excellence of its construction. This 'pepperpot' monument stands fifteen feet high in a scattering of stones, which appear to be mason's discards. It is unlikely that the stones, used and unused, are native to the hilltop since the turf and heather roundabout are undisturbed. Only by human effort can they have been carried here. There is an inscription carved on a tablet, over which the inevitable initials of visitors have been superimposed: its message cannot now be deciphered with certainty. The monument commemorates Alexander Padon, a Scottish Covenanter who held religious meetings in this lonely place, far from the long arm of persecution and, according to legend, every worshipper was required to bring one stone to each service—presumably for the building of the obelisk that became Alexander Padon's monument after his death and gave his name to the hill. This version of the erection of the monument has been disputed.

The monument on Padon Hill

Apart from the monument, there is little of immediate interest along the barren ridge, but a redeeming feature is the distant view northwards to the long line of the Cheviot Hills, over which lies the final stage of the Pennine Way. There is a very real satisfaction in this view—the last lap is in sight, the fulfilment of effort, the realisation of an ambition. At this moment, when the Cheviots first appear in the haze of distance, Edale seems a long long way behind, both in days and miles. It is, however, too early yet to start cheering, and any feeling of triumphant achievement is premature: the toughest assignment of all is yet to be faced.

It is quite easy to follow the route beyond Padon Hill, a continuous fence being a reliable guide to the next height of Brownrigg Head, 1191 ft, a dreary upland remarkable only for its many boundary stones. Here a wide prospect of the valley of Redesdale is revealed, much of it afforested, with the endless miles of the Cheviots beckoning beyond.

Redesdale from Padon Hill

Below *View east from Padon Hill*

The entrance to Redesdale Forest at Rookengate

A fence goes down north-west from Brownrigg Head to Rookengate, where the Gib Shiel road is joined at the entrance to Redesdale Forest. The road is then followed down to the valley, a fast and foolproof descent but in the close confinement of conifers for five miles. This is the official route.

The members of the Northern Area of the Ramblers' Association take pride in the fact that much of the Pennine Way lies within their home territory and have been active in suggesting certain improvements to the original official line of the route on both sides of Redesdale, their argument being that a better course is available on existing rights of way that keep to the open country instead and would obviate the lengthy section of road- and forest-walking. Their representations have in part succeeded, resulting in the diversion over Padon Hill and Brownrigg Head in lieu of the road walk via Gib Shiel to Rookengate, but they wanted also to have the route continued from Brownrigg Head by skirting the eastern boundary of the forest. This latter alternative, however, has been rejected, although having much to commend it, and walkers are committed to the long march through the trees from Rookengate.

Easy though the walking is from Rookengate, the sameness of the surroundings and absence of interesting features make the miles seem long, but at last the farm buildings of Blakehopeburnhaugh come into sight, signalling the end of tedium.

'Blake' is a common place name in Northumberland;

'hope' means a sheltered valley;

'burn' means a hill stream;

'haugh' means flat land beside a river.

Put together, they form the longest single place name on the Pennine Way.

Beyond Blakehopeburnhaugh is the River Rede and the farm's road bridge which gives direct access to the A.68. After crossing the bridge, the Way turns left and continues along the river bank to another farm with a long name, Cottonshopeburn Foot, also having access to the A.68 which is still ignored by the official route.

Cottonshopeburn Foot

The mile from Cottonshopeburn Foot to Byrness along the north-east bank of the river was under contention by the land-owners and tenants for some time after the Pennine Way was declared open, there being no right of way through the fields and no provision made for stiles. Although these deficiencies have been remedied, it is still much better to cross the river at Cottonshopeburn Foot by a bridge and follow a pleasant wooded lane that leads into Byrness without hindrance and provides a sylvan end to the day's march. Some shy and graceful creatures with white bob tails may be seen hereabouts: they are not big rabbits but roe deer.

The River Rede

Byrness is an important stage of the Pennine Way, none more so. An overnight stay here is essential, the morrow's walk being extremely strenuous. There is not much of Byrness: a small church, a licensed hotel, a Youth Hostel and cottages, and a café in which Pennine Wayfarers will be mightily interested alongside a filling station in which they will not, and half a mile up the road and off-route is a forestry village of forty-seven dwellings. The road is the fast and busy A.68 (Edinburgh–Newcastle), which carries a bus service. Byrness Hotel is open all the year round: wise virgins will book their rooms in advance and a telephone call from Bellingham may do the trick. And early to bed must be the order of the evening.

Byrness: hotel and church

The Cheviot Hills form a lofty barrier along the Scottish border, the range extending north-east from Newcastleton in Liddisdale to Wooller in Northumberland, a distance of forty straight miles, and at only one place, Carter Bar, does the high skyline relent to admit the passage of a motor road, the A.68. All else is a wild and lonely upland, grassy where not afforested and providing a vast sheep pasture. The hills are smooth in outline, the main ridge being supported on both sides by many miles of rolling foothills pierced by deep valleys.

Byrness, midway along the range, is in the Redesdale gap used by the A.68, and from it the Pennine Way climbs immediately to commence a switchback high-level traverse of the northern section. Walking conditions are rough but not difficult, nor is route-finding a problem thanks to the border fence that runs along the ridge for most of the way and serves as a guide. The problem lies in the distance that must be covered between breakfast and nightfall, twenty-nine miles of wilderness walking without a habitation or a road or shelter. This is the final stage of the Pennine Way and the toughest. It is the one section above all others where tent-dwellers, walkers who carry their sleeping gear on their backs, score most heavily against the bed-and-breakfast softies.

Once fairly committed to the walk, it is easier to go on than to turn back or try to escape from the ridge by descending into any of the valleys on either side, many of which have only isolated farmsteads and many no dwellings at all; if such deviations are made, steps will have to be retraced next day to regain the ridge were it was left, adding many miles to the journey. Unless the weather becomes impossibly beastly, it is better to battle against the conditions than to seek a route of escape.

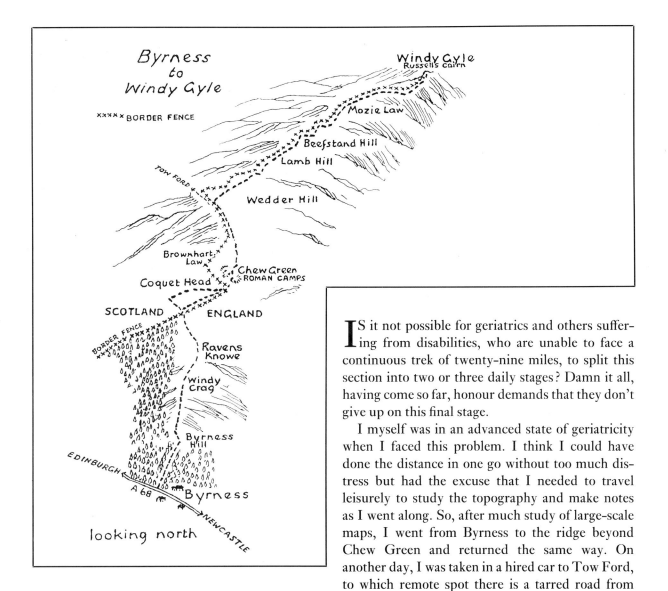

Byrness
to
Windy Gyle

××××× BORDER FENCE

Windy Gyle
Russell's cairn

Mozie Law

Beefstand Hill

Lamb Hill

Tow Ford

Wedder Hill

Brownhart Law

Chew Green
ROMAN CAMPS

Coquet Head

SCOTLAND   ENGLAND

BORDER FENCE

Ravens Knowe

Windy Crag

Byrness Hill

EDINBURGH

A 68   Byrness

NEWCASTLE

looking north

IS it not possible for geriatrics and others suffering from disabilities, who are unable to face a continuous trek of twenty-nine miles, to split this section into two or three daily stages? Damn it all, having come so far, honour demands that they don't give up on this final stage.

I myself was in an advanced state of geriatricity when I faced this problem. I think I could have done the distance in one go without too much distress but had the excuse that I needed to travel leisurely to study the topography and make notes as I went along. So, after much study of large-scale maps, I went from Byrness to the ridge beyond Chew Green and returned the same way. On another day, I was taken in a hired car to Tow Ford, to which remote spot there is a tarred road from Hownam on the west side, and from there walked up a grass path for two miles to the point on the ridge previously reached, and continued the Way over Windy Gyle to an ancient track which crossed the ridge. I descended this to the farm of Cocklawfoot, where I had asked the car to await my arrival at 6 p.m. The vehicle was there all right but turned out to be a Land Rover, which took me several miles into Town Yetholm. The Land Rover was a good idea and I chartered it for the following day when it took me not merely to Cocklawfoot but further up the bumpy track to the ridge where I had left it the previous day. Then it was a comfortable walk to Kirk Yetholm and journey's end.

With prayers for a fine day answered and a ruck-sack stuffed with thirst quenchers and emergency rations, the punishing task of walking along the tops of the Cheviot Hills to Kirk Yetholm is started by ascending a broad forest ride west of the Byrness Hotel, this being the steepest part of the day's walk. Above the trees, the summit of Byrness Hill is reached at 1358 ft. Enclosed by a fence, here was a fire look-out tower (now sadly demolished) and ancillary equipment. There is also a splendid lookout over the valley of Redesdale, with Padon Hill seen overtopping the vast plantations and a comprehensive view of the course of the River Rede and the pleasant Northumberland countryside.

Strange objects on Byrness Hill

Redesdale from Byrness Hill

A well-defined ridge forms beyond Byrness Hill, swelling to the minor heights of Saughy Crag, Houx Hill and Windy Crag before culminating in the cairned summit of Ravens Knowe, 1729 ft, overlooking a wide area of moorland used as the artillery range of a nearby military camp. Further, from Ogre Hill, Scotland comes into close view at last on the far side of the border fence at Coquet Head, the path descending alongside the boundary of the artillery range and a succession of warning notices to keep out and that firing is in progress when red flags are flying.

The summit of Ravens Knowe

Coquet Head

Scotland at last: the border fence at Coquet Head

The border fence is reached at a gate with notice boards, and it is a great moment for walkers as they pass through and set foot on Scottish territory. There is no sign, however, of the bonny banks and braes, the pretty glens and the grand mountains one is led to associate with Scotland in countless ballads: here are only harsh moors of rank grass and dreary desolation—and ground just as soggy as England. But it is exciting to step from one country into another and so reach a major milestone on the journey.

The official route now makes a short detour up the hillside before returning to the border fence, an unnecessary deviation, and most walkers prefer a short cut by keeping alongside the fence, passing more notices emphasising that the English side is a prohibited area, and crossing a trickle of water that becomes the River Coquet. When the fence turns sharply west, there, just beyond, are the earthworks of the Roman camps of Chew Green, the route passing between them.

The Roman camps and forts at Chew Green occupy an unlikely site and it is a surprise to find such extensive ramifications in a dreary setting on a low hillside encompassed by lofty moors on all sides except where the Coquet has carved a valley through the eastern foothills. The camps were built beside Agricola's road from York to Scotland, known as Dere Street and were extensive, covering an area of about fifty acres. When explored at ground level, their pattern seems complicated, and only in aerial views are the rectangular outlines clearly seen. Star markers indicate the principal earthworks. Among the crumbled remains, sections of the ramparts are still well defined and it is obvious from a walk around the perimeter that this was one of the largest and most important of the Roman military establishments in Britain.

In recent years, the present-day army authorities have constructed a motor road almost up to this point to serve their artillery ranges. This road comes from the east along the line of Dere Street, so that it is possible, but only with their approval, to reach the site by car and thus break the journey along the Pennine Way. This is the only place on the Way along the whole length of the Cheviots that access by car is possible.

The Roman camp at Chew Green

Dere Street skirts the eastern fringe of the camps and the Pennine Way adopts it for the next part of the walk, rejoining the border fence after a gradual ascent. Over the fence and reached through a gate is a Roman Signal Station, where there is a first view of the hills and valleys on the west side of the ridge. From the fence hereabouts, the valley of the River Coquet can be seen winding through the eastern foothills but with no hint of its later beautiful scenery around Rothbury.

The fence is kept alongside to level ground at the top of the ridge, where a grass path veers off to the left and descends for two miles to Tow Ford, a lonely spot with the advantage of a tarred road to Hownam, a village four miles further.

Now the border fence deserts the Pennine Way, going off north-west intent on adhering strictly to the watershed and for almost two miles the Way is without its reassuring company. A beeline has to be made across a featureless plateau with only an occasional post to mark the passage: this section is the worst to negotiate in mist. It will be appreciated here that the difficulties of steering a course along the Cheviots without the comfort of the fence would be immense, the ridge having none of the characteristics of a true ridge and being broad and undulating and lacking landmarks. It is a relief when the fence comes back and continues alongside.

The valley of the River Coquet

Looking along the ridge to Lamb Hill

With the fence again serving as a guide, there will be no further problems of route-finding for many miles ahead: there could not be a more reliable companion than this modest post-and-wire boundary marker. It now continues without a break along the ridge and over the highest Cheviots, the Way following slavishly as though afraid to deviate and lose sight of it.

As the ridge narrows somewhat, it becomes clear that it forms a definite watershed. Streams flowing eastwards from it join the River Coquet down gentle slopes, ultimately entering the North Sea at Amble; further along they flow into the River Breamish to reach the sea at Bamburgh, while all west-flowing streams are destined for the River Tweed at Kelso.

It was along this central part of the northern Cheviots that I experienced the strangest weather conditions I have ever known. Tow Ford was gloomy as I left the car I had chartered, but the sky brightened as I climbed the two miles up to the border fence, which I found bathed in bright sunshine under a cloudless sky: a remarkable transformation. For eight miles I walked along the ridge enjoying brilliant weather, but I became increasingly aware that the valleys on both sides were becoming obscured in a shroud of dark clouds; on the west side particularly they became enveloped in inky blackness, a frightening contrast to the sunlit ridge. It was as though I was walking along the crest of a rainbow rising from a dark and hostile sea. The ridge stretching before me was starkly clear but all else was covered by an impenetrable black mask. I walked alone in a world of my own. Conditions improved after I had passed over Windy Gyle and descended to the farm of Cocklawfoot, where the Land Rover was awaiting me. It was then I learned that there had been a violent rainstorm in the area for many hours, the downpour being the most severe my driver could remember.

The summit of Lamb Hill looking to Beefstand Hill

The six miles of the ridge to Windy Gyle lack interest and are more satisfactorily illustrated by photographs than described in words. The fence undulates over the summits of Lamb Hill, 1677 ft, Beefstand Hill, 1842 ft, and Mozie Law, 1812 ft, with the Pennine Way faithfully following suit. An absence of landmarks, other than unnecessary P.W. signs, makes this section a monotonous treadmill. Conditions underfoot are fairly good: there are some wet places but the ground is generally dry and vegetated by grass and heather with an occasional sighting of the lovely cloudberry.

View from Lamb Hill

Looking north-east from Beefstand Hill

Below *The Rowhope Valley from Mozie Law*

The solitary walker on the Cheviots has an intense feeling of loneliness and isolation, much more so than on Kinder Scout or the Cross Fell range, largely due to the extensive area of foothills on all sides, these rising in waves one after another and forming the horizon in every direction. They completely shut out visual contact with centres of population and lines of communication. The landscape is primeval, untouched and unsullied. A few shepherds' tracks cross the ridge; otherwise, the path scraped by two decades of walkers and the few posts and cairns that guide their steps are the only signs that others have been here since the men who erected the border fence long ago. Generations of sheep have grazed these wild uplands without disturbance.

Windy Gyle from Mozie Law

Beyond Mozie Law, the fence turns sharply east, obeying the watershed, and the path turns with it to climb gradually to the top of Windy Gyle, 2034 ft, the highest point so far reached on the day's walk and the highest summit attained since leaving Cross Fell.

Russell's Cairn, Windy Gyle

Windy Gyle is midway between Byrness and Kirk Yetholm and those who arrive here in a state of near exhaustion will find no comfort in the fact that the second half of the day's walk is tougher to negotiate than the first. They will feel sympathy for the prehistoric men who carried up the stones that form a huge tumulus on the summit. This giant pile is known as Russell's Cairn and is said to commemorate a Lord Russell who was slain in 1585 during a dispute, but is more likely to be a Bronze Age burial mound.

The Cheviot, from Russell's Cairn

Windy Gyle is a superb viewpoint, both retrospectively over the ridge just traversed and forward to the continuation of the Way, the next four miles being clearly in sight backed by the highest of all Cheviot summits, the Cheviot itself with an altitude of 2676 ft.

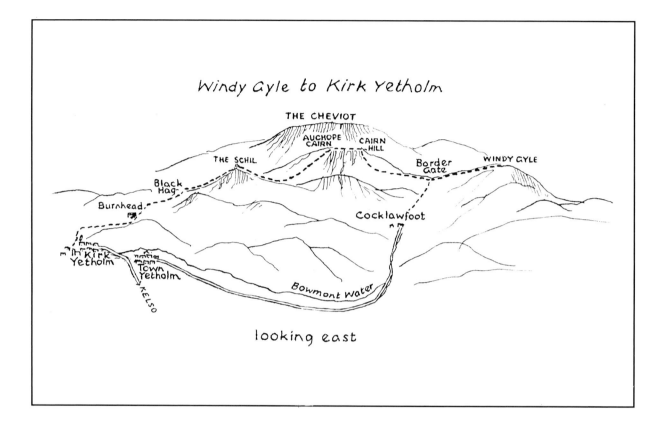

FROM Russell's Cairn, the path keeps to the Scottish side of the fence for the first and only time, descending gradually to a slight depression and passing another tumulus with a star marker, this also being a large mound of stones and thought to be the original Russell's Cairn.

An old road, now grassy, crosses the depression and passes through a gate in the fence known as the Border Gate. This old road has the name of Clennell Street and is probably a medieval trade route from Cocklawfoot to upper Coquetdale.

One should consider the hours of daylight remaining at this stage, the weather and the condition of the blisters. It is the only chance of escape from the ridge before the end of the Pennine Way at Kirk Yetholm, still fourteen arduous miles and six long hours distant. From here, Clennell Street goes distinctly down to the farm of Cocklawfoot, from which there is a road along the Bowmont Valley for seven miles to the comforts of Town Yetholm. This is clearly a deviation to be adopted only in dire emergency as the whole distance would have to be retraced to Border Gate the next day in order to continue the Way—a formidable undertaking unless transport can be hired for the return to Cocklawfoot; this is another case where carriers of tents score an advantage. This was the occasion that I arranged for the Land Rover to take me back all the way to the Border Gate the next morning: a bumpy ride but a great saving in energy for ancient legs.

Strong walkers will scorn the option offered by Clennell Street and pass through the Border Gate to continue the journey on the English side of the fence, surmounting three subsidiary summits—Butts Road, 1718 ft, King's Seat, 1743 ft, and Score Head, 1910 ft—on a long climb to the roof of the Cheviots at the west top of Cairn Hill at 2419 ft. The later stages of the ascent are cruelly laborious over rough ground pitted with peat hags which seriously retard progress by causing endless trial-and-error deviations. To meet such difficulties underfoot after all the hardships and tribulations already endured during the day's walk is too unkind for words, other than profane oaths, but a desire for survival keeps the boots plodding upwards and in due course the west top of Cairn Hill is reached at an acute angle in the fence.

The Cheviot from the fence on Cairn Hill

Directly ahead from this point is the highest of all these hills, the Cheviot, 2676 ft, seen across an uninviting morass of peat and bog a long mile away to the north-east. Its ascent is an optional extra to the official route, which here turns sharply north-west with the fence, but it is really asking too much to include it in the itinerary of a very long day's walk. Supermen may take it in their stride, but lesser mortals are better advised to leave it alone and apply their efforts to completing the Pennine Way, reserving the Cheviot for a separate expedition sometime in the future.

The acute angle in the fence on Cairn Hill, and therefore the acute angle in its faithful follower, the path, mark the start of the final stage of the journey, the 'homeward' march to Kirk Yetholm. The fence no longer drifts in an easterly direction but, as though suddenly deciding to get the whole thing over and done with, turns resolutely north-west, heading for the ultimate destination.

Cairn Hill is the limit of the gathering grounds of the River Coquet. From here onwards, streams flow north into Scotland; down on the left are tributaries of the Bowmont Water and a reference to the map reveals this as the river that flows through Yetholm, another encouraging indication that the end is near.

After a last look back to the southern horizon and the rolling uplands so far traversed and which now pass from sight, the Way continues over easier ground to the next height, Auchope Cairn, 2382 ft, which has a collection of 'stone men' and commands a wide prospect over the terrain still to be crossed, the foothills now being seen to be descending to the Tweed basin. Except for the rise to a final summit, the Schil, the trend is downhill.

'Stone men' on Auchope Cairn

Hen Hole

Almost immediately after leaving the summit of Auchope Cairn, a spectacular sight is revealed by a short detour from the fence to look down into the narrow ravine of Hen Hole, a tremendous chasm uncharacteristic of the Cheviots. Sheer cliffs, defending the nesting sites of many birds, plunge to depths that never see sunlight yet, in rocky niches, shelter many rare varieties of flowering plants amongst the ferns and mosses: this is a favourite haunt of botanists. A stream originating on the Cheviot cascades down the ravine and enters a deep valley as College Burn.

No matter how tired the limbs, Hen Hole should not be passed unnoticed. It is the highlight of the day, fashioned by nature and too wonderful to be left unseen.

The summit of the Schil

Below *Auchope Cairn from the Schil*

A long descent on firm dry turf, a welcome change, goes down to a wide and heathery depression with little of interest apart from an exquisite view northwards along the valley of College Burn. Across the depression, the fence leads upwards to the rocky tor on the summit of the Schil, 1985 ft, which, alone amongst the Cheviot heights, has the appearance of a real mountain top.

From the stony crest of the Schil, where those fortunate enough to have sufficient energy left may indulge in some mild rock-climbing, a mile-long descent on grass leads to a depression, the border fence being superseded by a border wall midway down the slope. In the depression, below the minor hillock of Black Hag, one passes through a gate. This is a sad moment for sentimentalists, a place for farewells, because at this point the border is abandoned and the fence (now a stone wall) that has been so friendly a companion and so reliable a guide over the last twenty miles is left behind. Here the last steps on English soil (mud, actually) are taken, the remainder of the route being wholly in Scotland.

The Cheviot and the Schil from Black Hag

Bereft of the assistance of the fence, route-finding is again the responsibility of the walker, and almost at once, in confusing terrain, there is a possibility of going astray. From the gate, a track contours the slope to a col between Black Hag and a neighbouring height, the Curr, giving a last retrospective view of the Cheviot and the Schil before they are lost to sight. Over the col, the deepening valley of Curr Burn goes directly down to green fields: an obvious and inviting way off the hills but not the right one. Instead, the head of this valley is skirted to cross the marshy upper basin of Halter Burn and, as the path starts to descend through bracken, there is revealed ahead, at long last, the road to Kirk Yetholm threading through the Halterburn valley. The end is near. Victory is in sight.

Excitement is now running high. Feet are dragging, shoulders are sagging, the mouth gapes for nourishment and the limbs cry out in agony for a rest and a long sit down. Eyes strain for a first sight of Kirk Yetholm, but it is hidden by a low ridge and cannot yet be seen. The adrenalin is surging, the pulses racing. Only three more miles and the Pennine Way will have been well and truly conquered. Edale is a world away, and forgotten.

The slope is descended to the farm of Burnhead, the first habitation seen since leaving Byrness and, to prove that a return has in fact been made to civilisation, a television aerial sprouts from the farmhouse chimney. Television too has been forgotten during these past few weeks.

The Halterburn valley

The Border Hotel, Kirk Yetholm

Then the road is reached, and how strange it feels to walk on smooth tarmac after gingerly picking a way through tussocky grass, tough heather and gluey peat all day! The Halterburn valley is quiet, with little traffic; offers of lifts by overtaking cars will of course be rejected as a matter of honour. Alongside flows the Halter Burn, its banks bright with musk. Then, at a cattle grid, comes the last straw, a sight to cause dismay and despair for the road is here seen to rise steeply to the top of a hill and must be negotiated by weary bodies that have already been flogged more than enough. This is a cruel last lap, but it must be tackled, either by zigzagging from side to side to ease the gradient, or even on hands and knees if the legs rebel. But when the top is reached there is unbridled joy at the sight of Kirk Yetholm nestling below: the promised land at last. And the way to it, mercifully, is downhill.

Before entering the village, walkers who have been well brought up will smarten themselves and try to look presentable. Boots will be scraped clean, clothes in disarray made tidy, unruly hair plastered down and, above all, shoulders will be straightened and the body held proudly erect. Not that there will be a civic reception, or people lining the pavements. Nothing like that. Not even a WELCOME sign. The only recognition of a heroic achievement to be expected, provided certain conditions are fulfilled, is a free drink at the Border Hotel provided by a sympathetic benefactor.

Kirk Yetholm, once a haunt of gipsies, is a quiet village pleasantly set around a tree-shaded green and has a Youth Hostel, a church, a scattering of old cottages and a bus service to Kelso, with the Border Hotel the star attraction for walkers who have travelled 270 miles on foot from Edale.

Kirk Yetholm

The following paragraphs are quotes from the concluding page of *Pennine Way Companion* and are addressed to walkers arriving at Kirk Yetholm at the end of their marathon journey:

'You have completed a mission and achieved an ambition. You have walked the Pennine Way, as you dreamed of doing. This will be a very satisfying moment in your life. You will be tired and hungry and travel-stained. But you will feel great, just great.

'There is no brass band to greet you, there is nobody waiting to pin a medal on your breast. There may be people about but they will take no notice of you. Nobody cares that you have walked, and just this minute completed, the Pennine Way. You will not get your name in the papers, nor be interviewed for television. No, the satisfaction you feel is intensely personal and cannot be shared: the sense of achievement is yours alone simply because you have earned it alone. . . .

'Anyway, you didn't walk the Pennine Way to please other people. You did it because it was a challenge and you wanted to see if you could do it. You wanted to test yourself. You didn't do it to earn memories, but memories you will have, and in abundance, for the rest of your life, highlighting past days. You will find you have enriched yourself. You will be more ready to tackle other big ventures and more able to bring them to a successful conclusion. You have learned not to give up.

'Well done!'

AUTHOR'S NOTE IN CONCLUSION

Slight changes in the detail of the route of the Pennine Way occur frequently. These are of little consequence in the general description intended by this book, such as new signposts and cairns, improvements and minor deviations of footpaths, new opportunities for refreshments or accommodation along the route, and so on. A few additional Youth Hostels have been established at convenient halts.

A recent revision of the official route must be mentioned, however. Walkers who have not already done the walk but plan to do so, should note that the last few miles to Kirk Yetholm from Black Hag have been replanned, the route along the Halterburn valley as described in this book now being classified as a bad-weather alternative.

AWainwright

INDEX OF PLACE-NAMES

(End papers in hardback edition) Looking west at Winshields Crag: (Page i) Thwaite: (Pages ii—iii) The Pennine Way: (Page iv—v) Crowden